THE
DOCTOR'S
WIFE'S
THINKING
THIN
COOKBOOK

From the Kitchen of
the Formerly Fat Psychiatrist

THE DOCTOR'S WIFE'S THINKING THIN COOKBOOK

Eleanor Rubin

TRIDENT PRESS   New York   1967

Library of Congress Catalog Card Number: 67-23592

Published simultaneously in the United States and Can-
ada by Trident Press, a division of Simon & Schuster,
Inc., 630 Fifth Avenue, New York, N. Y. 10020.

PRINTED IN THE UNITED STATES OF AMERICA

Dedicated to
My Formerly Fat Psychiatrist

Contents

Foreword

Let me say again that fatness is an emotional sickness. The only way to lose weight is to diet. However, getting on a diet, staying there and sustaining the weight loss requires emotional know-how. I've tried to provide that know-how in my book, *The Thin Book by a Formerly Fat Psychiatrist*.

I hope you have consulted with your doctor. It is great foolishness to embark on a serious weight loss project without his help. If you are emotionally ready and have chosen "D" Day, I think you will find this book very helpful. It provides foods and recipes that will pleasantly satisfy the requirements of nearly any thinning diet. My wife is an expert. She's lived with a fat man for years—and she's helped him get thin and stay thin.

So think thin, eat thin and enjoy living.

T. I. R.

Introduction

Do you think that life has been difficult up to now? Have there been just too many emergencies, frustrations, conflicts, depressions mixed with periods of boredom and a feeling of purposeless living? That is all behind you. You are an official "companion." This means that someone very close to you has decided to start dieting. You may be companioning a husband, child, boss, parent, friend or yourself. Whoever the dieter may be, let me assure you that you have a gargantuan job, one that may make you look back with nostalgia at any past difficulties. The frustration of purposeless living is behind you: you're working to get your companion to lose weight and, even more important, to maintain the weight loss.

This is no small job if you are cooking for a family and don't want to spend your entire day in the kitchen cooking separate dishes for the dieter. If you're the boss's companion for eight hours a day you're sure to rate a bonus when you come up with some low-calorie snacks and lunches. If you have to be your very own companion, you are really in a most difficult position and surely will deserve *La*

Croix de Guerre when you have achieved your goal.

Frankly, I consider myself a veteran companion, having been through many campaigns these past twenty years. (Fortunately, my scars are not visible.) I have learned to anticipate certain behavior on the part of the dieter, can gauge how long it will take for each period of disgruntlement to pass and how to survive. I'll share these tidbits with you. You may find that you can use them, too, or they may spark you into finding your own way during crucial periods of dieting.

When your dieter solemnly announces that Diet Day has arrived, you must take him seriously (maybe this time he really means it). You take the positive approach because it just might catch on. Keep your sarcastic remarks inaudible, gather strength and rally to the challenge.

I cleared the kitchen of all the tempting high-calorie "poison" foods. That doesn't mean I threw them away. I just found suitable hiding places. Actually, the linen closet was my refuge, since I am the only one who opens that door. You'll have to discover your own. The diet began with the very next meal. This happened to be breakfast at our house, but whichever it may be, I have found that a hearty satisfying meal is of great benefit to the dieter. I served half a grapefruit, a small lean steak (or two small lamb chops or a lean hamburger) and coffee (or tea) with a non-caloric sweetener. Since I went to all that trouble to broil a breakfast, how could my dieter bear to be unfaithful for the remainder of the day.

From 9:00 to 5:00 the secretary-companion must come through with snacks and lunch. She can have no cookies hidden behind the typewriter or chocolate bars in the file under H. She'll come up with a noncaloric soda, tea or a low-calorie canned dessert or some chestnut honey treats (page 90) or a diet sandwich (pp. 9-10). A good lunch to have sent in would consist of a huge shrimp cocktail, tossed green salad with a minimum of his favorite dressing, a half cantaloupe with 2 tablespoons of cottage cheese and a beverage (tea, coffee). These foods must be served with utmost nonchalance and not as sacrifice food. During the late afternoon a small glass of tomato juice or buttermilk and some carrot sticks and celery sticks sprinkled with seasoned salt are sure to be just the thing to prompt him into suggesting that it's time to call it a day even though it is only 4:30 P.M.

Now, what have I been doing as the dieter's home companion? Have I been busy cooking, marketing, reading low-calorie recipes? No, I have been stuffing myself with all kinds of poison foods so that when we dine at night I will be completely lacking in appetite and can set a good example by eating minute quantities in front of my dieter. We shall have a cup of bouillon, a very crisp salad with chicken breast cacciatore, string beans, beets, a small glass of Chianti, followed by strawberries with low-calorie topping. This to be accompanied by gay conversation, light gossip and jokes despite the fact that I'm on the verge of nausea from my afternoon's gorgings.

This first day of dieting requires a little celebrating but not with friends. Just a movie, a walk along Fifth Avenue, doing the paperback galleries, or some T.V. and then early to bed. Tomorrow is going to be a hard day and we'll both need all the rest we can get to cushion ourselves for the next two weeks. (Part-time companions had better bolster themselves with plenty of rest for a most difficult two weeks ahead.)

After the first diet meal you can look forward to several emotional periods. The first one is that of enthusiasm. This may barely last through the first meal or it may extend for almost three days. Ride with it, however short it may be. It will wane, because dieting has not yet become a way of life and the dieter, having to constantly make choices about foods, soon becomes irritated with himself.

So the second phase of dieting comes into being. This is extreme irritation which will last at least

two weeks. During these two irritating weeks the
dieter will be suspicious and belligerent. Chances are
that he will show no visible weight loss and will ac-
cuse you of serving fattening foods (and after all
the trouble you've taken, too!). Take it nobly. Go
quietly into the bathroom, turn on the tub faucet
and cry and scream like a child. It's really great.
(Chances are he'll apologize later on.) He will continue to be unbearable, making an issue of the most
unlikely things: the knife is dull, the children are
too noisy, there aren't enough lamps in the house.
All of which have always been this way. The dieter
becomes increasingly unbearable and the companion must surely be an angel to survive some of
the abuse that is in store for her. Just keep remind-
ing yourself that this is only temporary. You will
get frequent apologies and just as frequent irrational
behavior. This is a good time to invite some close
friends over for small supper parties and feed them
all on the dieter's menu.

Believe it or not, you'll have three to five days of
peace when an initial drop in weight is established.
You may even receive a bouquet of flowers for the
occasion! Then back to some more irrationality
which may be followed by a binge. How depressing!
Chin up to both of you. All is not lost; continue dieting and don't even discuss the indiscretion. There
will be ups and downs from now on because the
dieter won't be losing weight at the super rate he
feels his supreme sacrifice merits. But you'll be able
to take it now because there's always the bathroom
to hide in, or that secret cache of Mallomars (my
pet kind of chocolate-covered marshmallow-filled
cookie) in the closet.

After a succession of plateaus and periods of
weight loss despite intermittent binges, the dieter
will at last be on his way toward his goal. By this
time he will also have established a new way of life:
that is, a sensible pattern of eating—and for this you
rate a bonus and a new fur hat!

THE
DOCTOR'S
WIFE'S
THINKING
THIN
COOKBOOK

Helpful Hints

Since I began cooking by keeping foremost and forever in mind the caloric values of every morsel that crosses my pan, I have developed some useful habits. I'll pass them on to you. Perhaps you, too, have already evolved similar diet-conscious cooking aids or perhaps they will stimulate your cooking pattern toward low-calorie creative cookery.

It is a good idea to invest in the new "coated" cookware if it is of good quality. Old-fashioned heavy iron pans are, I feel, equally as good. I have had a pair of award-winning (I get the awards from my family when I use them) black iron frying pans for sixteen years. I bought them at an auction at the insistence of my son who was then four years old. When my bid was accepted and we took the pans outside, he kept urging me to "try them out." Upon questioning him as to exactly what he wanted me to do with them, I realized that this was a case of mistaken identity. My youngster thought that the auctioneer was

1

selling "flying pans" and that was why he was so eager for me to buy them. They were, however, the best purchase I ever made.

In any case, whatever cookware you use, always warm it before adding butter or oil for frying. I pour in the quantity called for, swish it around and then pour it off into a little container to be used for the rest of the recipe. And if I can get away with less than is called for, I feel that I've won a minor victory.

As for cooking oils versus butter or margarine: there are times when you want the flavor of olive oil to come through in the recipe. For such dishes I use 1 teaspoon of olive oil and for the remainder of the oil called for, I use margarine or butter. Since oil has a higher caloric value than margarine or butter, I use it as seldom as possible. I also use margarine more frequently than butter in cooking because of the cholesterol factor. However, just as with the olive oil, there are times when a taste of butter is all-important, as, for example, with omelettes.

In this calorie-conscious cooking world of mine, I have become aware of how little flour is really needed for thickening sauces and coating meats. With the advent of the powdered variety of flour, it is easier to use less and get a good coating. My method of flouring is to combine all the spices with the specified amount of flour, spread it out on a board or large platter and pat the well-dried meat, fish or poultry onto the floured surface.

Needless to say, unadorned food is the lowest in calories. Unfortunately, the dieter soon tires of such food and the entire diet. So I have found it desirable to dress up ordinary foods with a few extra calories and thereby, perhaps, be instrumental in preventing or forestalling a binge.

Skimmed evaporated milk, used in many of the recipes in this book, can be purchased as such. If it is not available in your community, you can make a suitable substitute by adding to an envelope of nonfat powdered milk (1 quart size) enough water to make 12 ounces of liquid.

Low-calorie salad dressings have never worn well with us. We would have bursts of enthusiasm about a new product only to find that it had lost something the second time around. I now use any of my favorite regular dressings, but sparingly. Even so, when I offer a portion to the dieter, I give the salad an extra little shake before putting it on his plate.

I found it stimulating for myself and the dieter (we are oftentimes one and the same) to try one new recipe every day. This makes each meal a little more exciting. If the food happens to have a gourmet quality, don't be surprised to hear, "Say, are you sure this is dietetic? I've been dieting all day so don't make me spoil my record. Don't be a friendly enemy!" Don't fret over these remarks, they're complimentary!

New dishes, whether you have created them yourself or are following a recipe, can be an adventure. They can also be a diet aid if you have to be your own companion and you're a homemaker. I have found it helpful to invite a friend for lunch and try out a new diet specialty. Having a luncheon guest is always good for self-discipline (especially if you're almost ready for a binge). It's harder to cheat with someone watching.

I have found the powdered broths of all flavors (vegetable, beef and chicken) to be extremely useful as a spice. Add them liberally to your hamburger patties, vegetables, soups and seafood dishes. Try them. You'll find the flavoring quite good.

Whenever you're using herbs, onions or celery it is always best to use fresh foods rather than the dehydrated variety. They not only taste better but also add a little more bulk to the recipe rather than just flavoring. And low-calorie bulk is just what the dieter needs!

Hors d'Oeuvres

TRUDY'S CANAPÉ

Clean 8 to 12 carrots, depending on how many canapés you want to make. Slice the carrots crosswise, using only that portion that will give you a good-size disc. Slice them a shade thicker than "wafer" thin. Cover them with water and store in the refrigerator for a few hours before using.

These discs will be the base for your canapés. I suggest the following topping (which was my daughter's invention):

½ cup cottage cheese	caviar, capers, rolled an-
2 teaspoons sour cream	chovies, or seasoned
1 teaspoon chives	salt

Keep the cheese at room temperature for an hour and then put it through a sieve or blender so that it is creamed. Blend the cheese, sour cream and chives thoroughly. Spread this mixture on the carrot discs and top each disc with a drop of caviar, a caper, a rolled anchovy or just some seasoned salt.

The calorie content—negligible.

CAPE COD CLAM DIP

3 tablespoons small curd cottage cheese
1 tablespoon sour cream (optional)
1 cup well-drained minced clams
¼ teaspoon Worcestershire sauce
1 tablespoon minced chives or ¼ teaspoon onion powder
freshly ground pepper

If you use sour cream, blend it into the cheese first. Then add all the other ingredients and blend well. Chill for several hours and serve with carrot sticks, celery sticks or as a stuffing for celery or a topping for carrot or cucumber rounds.

The entire recipe contains 200 calories. You could even serve half of it on a bed of lettuce with cold pickled beets for a very low-calorie luncheon dish.

RIVIERA CRAB DIP

1 cup cottage cheese
1 can crab meat (7 ounces)
½ tablespoon lemon juice
1 tablespoon minced green pepper
1 tablespoon mayonnaise
½ teaspoon Dijon mustard
salt and freshly ground pepper to taste

Sieve the cottage cheese and then beat for a few minutes with a rotary beater (or put through a blender).

Chop the crab meat and blend all the ingredients together. Garnish with capers and parsley. Chill and serve with carrot and celery sticks.

The entire dip has 300 calories.

Incidentally, you can easily substitute minced clams for the crab meat.

SHRIMP FOR HORS D'OEUVRES

1½ pounds shrimp cooked, shelled and deveined
1 cup lime or lemon juice
½ cup chopped onions
1 teaspoon salt
½ teaspoon freshly ground pepper

Split the shrimp lengthwise and wash and dry them. Combine the lime or lemon juice and the onions with the shrimp and refrigerate for at least 4 hours. Season before serving.

Of course, this is not only good for the cocktail hour but also a handy snack for the nighttime nibbler. There are about 10 calories per shrimp, but the dieter doesn't have to eat all of them.

ITALIAN SHRIMP

1 cup wine vinegar	1 tablespoon mixed
½ cup olive or salad oil	pickling spices
3 cups water	1 teaspoon salt
1 large onion, sliced	2 pounds shrimp, shelled
	and deveined

Combine all ingredients but the shrimp in a saucepan and bring to a boil. Add the shrimp and cook 5 minutes. Pour into hot sterilized jars, cool and store in the refrigerator for at least 24 hours.

This is a superb emergency food, BUT it must be served well drained. The 8 portions from this recipe, which can also be used as an appetizer with cocktails or as the first course at dinner, will come to 180 calories each.

℞: SHRIMP BUTTERMILK DIP

1 5-ounce can shrimp	salt and pepper
¾ cup buttermilk	1 teaspoon prepared
1 tablespoon sour cream	horseradish
¼ cup chili sauce	¼ teaspoon Worcester-
1 tablespoon lemon juice	shire sauce

Drain the shrimp and chop them very fine. Mix with the remaining ingredients, or process in a blender until the shrimp are finely minced. Serve cold as a dip for celery, carrot or cucumber sticks.

The entire recipe makes about 1½ cups and has 350 calories.

Sandwiches

Sandwiches may have been invented by an Englishman, but I don't think they are respected more by any other nation than the United States. The sandwich has become so very much a part of our way of life that you only seem to become aware of it in its absence. For example, when you're dieting. What can you have for lunch if you can't eat bread? You can eat the same fillings on a plate with a fork and knife, but it certainly isn't as gratifying. There is something very satisfying about biting into a substantial conglomeration of bread-buffeted foods. The same foods forked and knifed simply don't taste the same.

I think that I've solved the problem somewhat.

In our house we use cheese in place of bread and vary the fillings as we would with any ordinary sandwich. I know that gourmet cheese lovers will shudder at this: the cheese, however, must be left uncovered in the refrigerator so that it dries out a bit and becomes firm. Then for a carbohydrate-free sandwich meal you can use the following fillers:

Swiss cheese with ham, mustard, tomato and lettuce: 335 CALORIES.

Sweet Muenster cheese with chicken brushed with Russian dressing, dill pickle and lettuce: 300 CALORIES.

American cheese brushed with mayonnaise, sliced egg, capers, lettuce and tomato: 280 CALORIES.

Swiss cheese with ½ tart apple, peeled and sliced: 250 CALORIES.

Edam with English mustard (or Dijon), sliced meat loaf and lettuce: 350 CALORIES.

American cheese with cottage cheese with seasoned salt, sliced Bermuda onion, tomato, cucumber, green pepper slivers and lettuce: 250 CALORIES.

Sweet Muenster cheese with tuna fish salad, sliced radishes and lettuce: 300 CALORIES.

Swiss cheese with roast beef, sliced pickled beets, Bermuda onion and lettuce: 350 CALORIES.

This list is incomplete and is limited only by your imagination.

Soups

SYL'S INSTANT VEGETABLE SOUP

2 cups chicken broth
2 cups water
1 teaspoon creole seasoning
¼ cup canned kernel corn
2 tablespoons chopped onion

½ cup diced celery
1 tablespoon minced parsley
2 chicken bouillon cubes
2 cups canned tomatoes
½ cup sliced okra
1 tablespoon uncooked rice

salt and pepper to taste

Mix all the ingredients together, bring to a boil and then simmer for 20 minutes. Taste for seasoning. And there is your instant soup! Only you will know how long it took to prepare. These 6 portions have 41 calories each.

CREAM OF CHICKEN SOUP

1 quart skimmed milk
1 3-ounce jar of chicken or ½ cup leftover chicken, cubed
5 chicken bouillon cubes
1 tablespoon minced instant onion

1 package black dehydrated mushrooms (optional)
2 tablespoons powdered flour
black pepper to taste
1 tablespoon minced dill

11

Warm the milk with the chicken. When the milk begins to simmer, add the bouillon cubes, After they have dissolved, add the onion and mushrooms and slowly add the flour, stirring continuously until the mixture begins to thicken; season with the pepper and add the dill. This recipe will serve 6.

This soup is perfect for an afternoon snack, to send along in a Thermos and even as a "company" dish. Best of all, there are only 52 calories per portion.

COLD CUCUMBER SOUP

3 medium-sized cucumbers
4 cups chicken bouillon
1 cup buttermilk
2 teaspoons fresh chopped dill
⅛ teaspoon fresh pepper

Peel the cucumbers, slice them in half lengthwise and remove all the seeds. Dice them and put them in a saucepan with boiling bouillon. Cook over a low flame for 10 minutes. Remove and purée by pushing through a sieve or put through a blender. Cool and then blend with the buttermilk, dill and freshly ground pepper. Correct the seasonings and serve well chilled.

This pleasantly cooling summer soup will serve 6 at 30 calories each.

TOMATO SOUP MADRILENE

4 cups beef bouillon
4 cups tomato juice
1 teaspoon sugar
½ cup sliced onion
2 sprigs parsley
2 celery stalks
2 cloves
2 tablespoons dry sherry
paprika
thin slices of lemon

Combine all the ingredients *except* the sherry, paprika and lemon. Bring them to a boil and cook over low heat for 20 minutes. Then strain and taste for seasoning. When you are ready to serve, warm the soup with the sherry and garnish each bowl with a sprinkling of paprika and a lemon slice.

This light soup is very easy to make and is an excellent emergency food. There are 8 cups of soup in this recipe and each one contains 40 calories.

GELID TOMATO SOUP MADRILENE

This is essentially the same as the warm variety. Follow the regular madrilene recipe, but add to it 2 envelopes of gelatin dissolved in ¼ cup cold water. Stir the dissolved gelatin into the hot soup until well mixed. Chill. Serve in chilled cups.

If you add a little more sherry, you can also serve this instead of a cocktail on a hot and tiring day.

MADRILENE CAVIAR GOURMET

For this, I start with the gelid madrilene recipe. When it is ready to be chilled, divide it into 8 serving cups. Into each, stir 1 teaspoon of caviar and chill. When you are ready to serve, drop 1 teaspoon of sour cream on top and put some chopped chives on top of the sour cream.

Of course, this increases the number of calories in the basic recipe and now each of 8 portions is 81 calories. But it's worth it!

CREAM OF MUSHROOM SOUP

1 pound mushrooms	¼ teaspoon white pepper
1 tablespoon butter	½ cup skimmed evapo-
2 tablespoons minced	rated milk (page 3)
onion	fresh parsley or
2 tablespoons flour	fresh dill
4 cups chicken bouillon	

Wash and drain the mushrooms. Chop the stems and half of the caps. Slice the remaining caps thin. Melt the butter in a preheated pan and sauté the onions and chopped mushrooms. Steam them covered for 3 minutes and then uncovered for about 5 minutes. Blend in the flour; add the bouillon, stirring steadily until it comes to a boil. Add the sliced mushrooms and pepper; cook over low heat for 15 minutes. Mix in the milk, taste for seasoning and sprinkle with fresh parsley or dill.

This is my favorite, a marvelous soup, satisfying and elegant enough to serve for company. It will serve 8 at 47 calories each.

CLEAR MUSHROOM SOUP

½ pound mushrooms
1 cup beef broth (consommé)
5 cups beef bouillon
sherry to taste

Slice the mushrooms, using the caps and the stems. Mix and heat the consommé and bouillon; then add the mushrooms and simmer for 30 minutes. (Isn't that a cinch!) Just before serving, spoon about 1 teaspoon of sherry into each cup, fill with the soup and serve. Six cold hungry people can have a light snack or appetizer for only 30 calories each (you can afford to offer your dieter a second helping!).

JAPANESE CLAM SOUP

24 steamer clams
2 cups chicken bouillon
2 cups clam juice
3 tablespoons finely chopped scallions
2 tablespoons minced parsley
2 tablespoons soy sauce
1 tablespoon sake or dry sherry

Scrub the clams and wash them thoroughly. Bring the bouillon and clam juice to a boil; drop the clams and scallions into it and cook over medium heat until the clams open. Stir in the parsley, soy sauce and sake or sherry. Let soup settle again before serving.

Each of 4 servings of this marvelous dish is 72 calories. If you aren't your own companion, dunk a piece of crusty white bread into the soup before you serve it to the dieter.

Salads

GREEN BEAN AND CARROT SALAD

1 can whole string beans (large size can)	2 tablespoons oil
4 carrots cut in julienne strips	1 tablespoon wine vinegar
	½ red onion
	salt and pepper

1 teaspoon capers

Drain the string beans thoroughly, pat dry and chill. Cook the carrots in a small amount of water so that they are tender but still crisp (you have to watch the pot here!). Chill. Mix the oil and vinegar. Slice the onion wafer-thin. Toss the beans, carrots and onions together with salt and pepper. Pour the oil and vinegar over and toss lightly. Sprinkle capers on top. Delicious! And it looks pretty, too.

Serves 6 for 55 calories each.

JENNIE'S STRING BEAN SALAD

½ pound fresh string beans	1 small onion, minced
1 tablespoon oil	2 hard-boiled eggs
	salt and pepper to taste

17

Clean and cook the string beans until they are tender, but not soft. Drain them first in a sieve and then on clean toweling. (You may even pat them dry.) Warm a small frying pan and then pour in the oil. Sauté the minced onion slowly in the oil until the onion becomes golden brown (do not use up too much of the 1 tablespoon of oil). When the onions are golden, remove the pan from the heat. Chop the eggs and the well-drained beans, season with salt and pepper, add the onions and oil, and refrigerate. This is a great luncheon main dish for 2 or a side dish for 4, particularly in the summer. As a side dish for 4, the calorie count is 80.

CABBAGE SALAD

3 cups shredded cabbage   1 carrot, shredded
1 teaspoon salt   1 green pepper, chopped
1 turnip, shredded   ¼ teaspoon dill seed
            Buttermilk dressing (page 24)

Cover the cabbage with salt and let it stand for 45 minutes; then wash and dry the cabbage thoroughly. (Drain it and actually squeeze the water out with your hands.) Toss all the other ingredients with the cabbage and moisten with the dressing. Chill. Serves 6 for 26 calories without the dressing.

CABBAGE RELISH

scant ½ cup horseradish   1 small head of cabbage,
sugar substitute equal to 1   shredded (about 4 cups)
   cup sugar   6 large beets, chopped
2 cups wine vinegar   dash of pepper and nutmeg

Mix all the liquids and spices until they are well blended. Toss the shredded cabbage and the chopped beets together. Pour the dressing over the cabbage-beet mixture and refrigerate.

Serve well chilled. This is an excellent accompaniment for boiled beef.

Итпараллельно

This recipe will serve 8 at 21 calories each.

CAPE COLESLAW

1 cup buttermilk
1 tablespoon mayonnaise
1 tablespoon sour cream
1½ teaspoons lemon juice
1 small onion, diced
pepper and salt to taste
1 small head of cabbage, shredded (about 4 cups)

Whip or whisk buttermilk, mayonnaise, sour cream and lemon juice. Add the onion and spices, and blend well. Pour over the cabbage, mix and refrigerate. This should be chilled for at least several hours, if not overnight.

This recipe will serve 6 nicely at only 55 calories per serving.

CREAMY CUCUMBER SALAD

2 tablespoons sour cream plus buttermilk to make up 1 cup of liquid
1 tablespoon wine vinegar
½ teaspoon salt
⅛ teaspoon fresh pepper
1 large cucumber
2 tablespoons chopped onion

Blend the sour cream, buttermilk, vinegar, salt and pepper with a wire whisk or rotary beater and set aside. Wash the cucumber and run a fork down its length all around. Slice in ¼-inch rounds. Marinate and chill with the onions in the buttermilk mixture for at least 30 minutes before serving. This is very good to have on hand for evening snacks. As a salad it serves 4, and each serving contains only 44 calories. It is also good for lunch with tuna fish mixed with cottage cheese. This lunch is convenient to take along to business for yourself (or your boss!).

CUMIN CUKES

1 cup buttermilk
1 tablespoon sour cream
3 medium cucumbers
½ teaspoon hot sauce (red hot)
1 teaspoon powdered cumin (or seeds)
1 tablespoon fresh dill
salt

Mix the buttermilk and sour cream and let them stand a while. Peel the cucumbers and grate them coarsely, or slice them very thin. Blend the spices with the milk mixture and add to the cucumbers. Refrigerate this dish for about 3 hours before serving.

This is something to have on hand as an emergency food. It is also good as a salad replacement when your dieter begins to complain.

The entire recipe contains 150 calories.

LEMON CUCUMBERS

2 cucumbers
¼ cup lemon juice
2 tablespoons snipped fresh dill
salt and freshly ground black pepper to taste

Peel and slice the cucumbers wafer-thin. Combine the remainder of the ingredients and pour over the cucumbers. Toss lightly and chill.

You don't even have to count the calories in this one!

ONION-CUCUMBER SALAD

2 onions
2 cucumbers
½ cup cider vinegar
¼ cup water
sugar substitute equal to 1 teaspoon sugar
1 teaspoon salt
¼ teaspoon freshly ground black pepper

Peel the onions and cucumbers and cut into paper-thin slices. Cover with salted ice water; cover and chill for 3 to 4 hours. Drain; add the vinegar, water, sweetener, salt and pepper. This serves 4 to 6, and you don't have to count the calories. It is another "free" food!

MARINATED CARROTS

1 16-ounce can carrots
2 tablespoons olive oil
2 tablespoons wine vinegar
2 cloves garlic, minced
¾ teaspoon salt
¼ teaspoon freshly ground black pepper
½ teaspoon oregano

Drain the carrots and place them in a dish. Mix together the oil, vinegar, garlic, salt, pepper and oregano. Pour over the carrots; marinate in the refrigerator for at least 4 hours.

Drain thoroughly before serving; each of 4 servings will then come to 60 calories.

OLD WORLD ROMANIAN EGGPLANT

1 medium eggplant	1 tablespoon lemon juice
½ cup minced onions	2 tablespoons salad oil

salt and freshly ground pepper to taste

The eggplant can be baked in the oven, either wrapped in foil or not; it may also be baked on top of the stove in a potato baker. However, I must warn you that if the eggplant is not wrapped, it may burst while baking and can be a bit of a nuisance to clean up. After about 45 minutes in a hot oven, the eggplant should be very tender. After it has cooled, peel it and mash it well; add the minced onion, lemon juice, oil, salt and pepper.

This mixture can be served as a relish accompaniment for a meat dish (warm or cold), cold with salad greens, or as an hors d'oeuvre. It can be served soon after it is prepared (at room temperature), but it is tastiest cold. It should not be reheated.

As a side dish for 6, each serving has 60 calories.

EGGPLANT RELISH VARIATION

To the preceding recipe, add ½ cup chopped fresh tomato and a dash of hot sauce. This increases the caloric value by 5 calories per portion but also makes for a heartier dish . . . as I mentioned earlier every little bit of bulk is welcome!

Dressings

HORSERADISH DRESSING

1 teaspoon dry mustard   1 cup buttermilk
2 tablespoons drained red   ½ teaspoon salt
  horseradish   2 tablespoons minced dill
             pepper to taste

Dissolve the mustard in 1 tablespoon water for 10 minutes. Mix all the ingredients together and beat with a wire whisk or fork. Refrigerate and serve as needed. The entire cup of dressing contains 80 calories.

This is good with cold leftover fish, on salads or over chopped raw vegetables.

PARSLEY DRESSING

1 tablespoon sour cream   ½ cup finely chopped
¾ cup buttermilk   dill pickle
3 tablespoons minced   ½ cup chopped tomatoes
  parsley   ¼ teaspoon salt

Blend the sour cream and buttermilk and let the mixture stand a while. Mix together the parsley, dill pickle, tomatoes and salt. Fold these

23

ingredients into the milk and cream mixture and chill.

Serve this with seafood. The entire recipe makes about 2 cups of dressing with a caloric count of 150.

GARLIC DRESSING

1 cup buttermilk   1 tablespoon sour cream
1 clove garlic, mashed   ¼ teaspoon dry mustard
       1½ teaspoons lemon juice

Beat all the ingredients with a rotary beater. Chill and then shake well before serving.

The entire recipe has 130 calories and can be used for fish or salad.

BUTTERMILK DRESSING #1

1 tablespoon mayonnaise   ¼ teaspoon garlic powder
½ cup buttermilk   1 tablespoon vinegar
pepper and salt   paprika

Blend all the ingredients together with a wire whisk or rotary beater. I use 1 tablespoon regular mayonnaise; if, however, you have found a palatable low-calorie mayonnaise, by all means use it and increase the amount to suit your own taste.

The entire recipe is 132 calories.

BUTTERMILK DRESSING #2

1 cup buttermilk   1 teaspoon Worcester-
¼ teaspoon salt   shire sauce
⅛ teaspoon pepper   dash of cayenne pepper
¼ teaspoon dry mustard 1 tablespoon vinegar
  in 1 tablespoon water   1 clove garlic, cut in half

Combine all ingredients in a jar. Shake vigorously and refrigerate. Remove the garlic before serving and shake vigorously again. This cup of dressing has 80 calories and is good for leftover cold fish and salads. If you add a little well-mashed blue cheese, it can even be used for a celery or carrot dip.

CUCUMBER DRESSING

1 cup finely chopped cucumber
¾ cup thick buttermilk
1 tablespoon sour cream
1 tablespoon lemon juice
1 tablespoon minced dill
½ teaspoon salt
freshly ground pepper

While the cucumbers are draining, mix the buttermilk, sour cream and lemon juice. Season the cucumbers with the spices and fold into the buttermilk mixture. Chill and serve. One and one-half cups of this dressing have 135 calories.

Seafood

SHELLFISH

BAKED MUSSELS

1 cup cooked chopped mussels	2 tablespoons minced celery
1 tablespoon onion	½ cup mussel broth
1 tablespoon fresh parsley	2 tablespoons bread crumbs
4 tablespoons chopped mushrooms	salt and pepper to taste
2 tablespoons Parmesan cheese	

The most difficult part of this recipe is the preparation of the fresh mussels. They have to be soaked in several changes of water; discard any mussels that float. You will need about 6 pounds of mussels to get 1 cup of cooked chopped mussels. Steam the cleaned, scrubbed mussels in a large covered pot with ¼ cup of dry white wine. The mussels will steam open in about 20 minutes. Let them cool and then remove the meat. You can reserve the largest shells for stuffing if you are going to serve the mussels as an hors d'oeuvre. Clean the dark mass from the mussel and chop the rest. If you can get water-packed

27

cooked mussels in your area, this recipe becomes an instant gourmet delight. If you use canned mussels, you can use some clam juice instead of the mussel broth. If you use fresh mussels, strain the broth several times through cheesecloth so that all the grit and sand are removed.

When you get the dirty work out of the way, mix everything together except the cheese. Taste before adding the salt. You can bake this mussel mixture in individual mussel shells, larger ramekins or in a shallow baking dish. Sprinkle the top with Parmesan cheese and broil for 10 minutes. The entire recipe is 360 calories, so divide it as you like.

MUSSELS STEAMED IN WHITE WINE

3 quarts cleaned mussels
½ cup white wine
3 cloves garlic, split
4 peppercorns
1 cup chopped fresh parsley
6 teaspoons butter

Follow the directions for the preparation of fresh mussels on page 27.

Steam the mussels in a mixture of the wine, garlic, peppercorns and parsley for about 10 minutes. Turn the mussels so that the ones on the bottom exchange places with the top ones.

When all the shells are opened (about another 5 minutes), the mussels are ready. Lift them out of the kettle and carefully spoon ½ cup of the liquor from the kettle into each soup bowl. Be careful not to dig down to the bottom when scooping out the liquor because there may be some sand. Add 1 teaspoon of butter to each bowl and then top it with the mussels. Dip the mussel meat into the mussel liquor and enjoy it! (If you're not dieting, you might try dipping some crusty French bread into the liquor, too.)

This recipe will give you enough to serve 6 as an appetizer at 90 calories each.

SHRIMP STROGANOFF

1 cup buttermilk	½ pound mushrooms,
1 tablespoon sour cream	sliced
1 large onion, minced	1½ pounds cooked shrimp
1 clove garlic, split	2 tablespoons seasoned
1 tablespoon butter	salt
2 tablespoons powdered flour	

Blend the buttermilk with the sour cream and set it aside, at room temperature. Fry the onions and garlic in ½ tablespoon of butter over a low flame until they are golden. Add the mushrooms and cook covered for 5 minutes. Drain the shrimp and pat dry. Mix the seasoned salt and the flour together. Spread the mixture out on a board or a platter and then place the shrimp on top, making sure that they become evenly coated. Remove the onions and mushrooms from the skillet, add the remaining butter and quickly toss the shrimp around in the pan over a medium heat. The coating on the shrimp should absorb the butter quickly and the shrimp will have a glossy appearance. Remove the garlic. Add the mushrooms and onions and the buttermilk/sour cream mixture and warm thoroughly. Do not boil. Serve immediately.

There are 4 portions in this recipe; each one has 238 calories.

QUICK GOURMET SHRIMP

2 tablespoons powdered flour	1 cup sliced canned mushrooms
2 tablespoons fresh chopped dill	1 teaspoon dried shallots
dash of paprika	1 cup skimmed evaporated milk (page 3)
1 teaspoon salt	2 tablespoons grated Cheddar cheese
1½ pounds cooked shrimp	
1 tablespoon margarine	

Mix the flour, dill, paprika and salt together.

Spread this out on a large board or platter. Drain
and dry the shrimp thoroughly. Spread them out
over the flour mixture and turn them several
times until they are evenly coated. Melt the
margarine in a preheated skillet, and toss in the
shrimp. Turn them frequently until they are
coated with margarine and appear glossy. At
this point, add the mushrooms, shallots and milk.
Warm them thoroughly. Sprinkle the cheese on
top. Cover and simmer for 1 minute—then it's
ready to serve.

There are 4 servings; each one has 261 calories.

SHRIMP AND MARINADE

2 pounds cooked, cleaned   2 tablespoons lemon juice
  shrimp   ¼ cup chopped fresh
3 large red onions, sliced   parsley
2 bay leaves, halved   2 teaspoons tarragon
1 lemon, thinly sliced   Tabasco sauce
4 tablespoons olive oil   ¼ cup capers
              salt and pepper to taste

Arrange the shrimp in a shallow dish and
alternate them with layers of onion and bay leaf
and lemon slices. Mix all the other ingredients
and pour over the layers. Cover and chill for 4
to 5 hours.

It is absolutely mandatory that the shrimp be
served *drained*. The 4 tablespoons of olive oil
contain 500 calories and our friend can do very
nicely without them! Also, don't leave it to him
to drain them as he is eating, for you and I know
that he has no willpower.

This is delicious as a before-dinner snack with
cocktails or as a luncheon main course.

Completely drained, the entire recipe is about
500 calories.

FAR EASTERN SHRIMP

1 tablespoon butter
4 sliced scallions
2 tablespoons soy sauce
½ teaspoon turmeric
¼ teaspoon ground
    cardamom
1 teaspoon salt

¼ teaspoon Tabasco sauce
1 cup bottled clam juice
1 teaspoon cornstarch
1 tablespoon water
1 pound raw shrimp,
    shelled and deveined

Melt the butter in a saucepan; sauté the scallions for 2 minutes. Add the soy sauce, turmeric, cardamom, salt, Tabasco sauce and clam juice. Cook over low heat for 10 minutes. Mix the cornstarch and water to a paste and stir into the hot mixture until thickened. Add the shrimp; cover and simmer for about 10 minutes.

This is shrimp with a slightly different flavor. There are about 3 servings of 220 calories each.

DILL SHRIMP

1½ pounds shrimp
3 tablespoons butter
Tabasco sauce to taste
½ teaspoon Worcester-
    shire sauce

2 teaspoons chopped fresh
    dill or 1 teaspoon dried
    dill weed
juice of ½ lemon

Shell and devein the shrimp and rinse them under cold running water. Melt the butter in a skillet large enough to hold the shrimp and, when it is heated, add them. Cook over moderate heat, covered, turning the shrimp once, until they are pink (about 3 to 5 minutes). Sprinkle the shrimp with Tabasco, Worcestershire, dill and lemon juice. Stir well and serve hot.

There is nothing dull about these dill shrimp.

Serve this to 4, and each portion will have 275 calories. (Keep frozen shrimp on hand and you'll never be stuck if you have unexpected dinner guests.)

CHINESE SHRIMP AND CHICKEN

2 tablespoons butter or
  margarine
2 cups coarsely chopped
  celery
1 cup sliced mushrooms,
  fresh or canned
1 small onion, diced

1 pound fresh raw shrimp,
  peeled
2 cups diced cooked
  chicken
1 teaspoon cornstarch
2 tablespoons soy sauce
½ cup frozen peas

salt and pepper to taste

Melt the butter or margarine in a skillet, add the celery, turn to coat with melted fat; cover the skillet and cook over low heat for 10 minutes. Add the sliced mushrooms, onion and the raw shrimp, and cook, covered, over low heat, until shrimp turn pink (about 10 minutes or so). Stir occasionally to prevent sticking. Add the diced chicken. Combine the cornstarch and soy sauce and add them to the mixture in the skillet. Next add the peas, salt and pepper. Stir well, then cook over medium heat until the peas are tender, the chicken is thoroughly heated and the sauce is thickened.

There are 257 calories in each of 6 portions.

PICKLED JUMBO SHRIMP

2 pounds jumbo shrimp
1 onion, sliced
1 carrot, sliced
2 tablespoons chopped
  parsley

small piece of bay leaf
juice of 2 lemons
6 ounces dry white wine
salt and pepper to taste

Shell and devein the shrimp. Put the remaining ingredients in a saucepan, bring to a boil and simmer for 1 minute. Add the cleaned shrimp, cover the pan and simmer until the shrimp have turned pink (about 7 minutes longer). Cool and refrigerate overnight in the marinade. To serve, remove the shrimp from the marinade and arrange on a platter; sprinkle with a few tablespoons of the marinade, and serve very cold.

These pickled shrimp will serve 6 at 208 calories each.

SHRIMP-STUFFED GREEN PEPPERS

6 green peppers
2 quarts plus 1 cup boiling water
12 tablespoons cooked rice
1½ cups chopped cooked shrimp
1 teaspoon grated onion
1 cup chopped fresh tomatoes

1 cup chopped mushrooms
1 teaspoon salt
¼ teaspoon freshly ground black pepper
½ clove garlic, minced
2 teaspoons curry powder
⅓ cup tomato paste
3 teaspoons butter

6 tablespoons fresh bread crumbs

Preheat the oven to 350°.

Cut a ¼-inch slice from the stem end of each pepper and remove the seeds. Place the peppers in a saucepan, add 2 quarts of boiling water, cover and steam for 5 minutes. Remove the peppers from the pan and drain them.

Mix the cooked rice with the shrimp, onion, tomatoes, mushrooms, salt, pepper, garlic, curry powder, remaining cup of water and the tomato paste. Mix thoroughly and fill the peppers with this mixture. Mix the butter with the bread crumbs and use to top the stuffed peppers.

Place the stuffed peppers in a baking dish and cook for 20 minutes.

Each of these peppers has 160 calories. Bet you can't eat just one!

SHRIMP MORNAY

1 tablespoon butter
1 tablespoon flour
1 cup clam or chicken broth
2 tablespoons grated sharp Cheddar cheese

¼ cup skimmed evaporated milk (page 3)
salt and freshly ground black pepper to taste
1 pound shrimp, cooked, shelled and deveined

2 tablespoons grated Parmesan cheese

Melt butter and blend in the flour. Gradually

stir in the broth. Bring to a boil, stirring. Next, stir in the Cheddar cheese until it melts. Add the milk and season to taste with salt and pepper.

Divide shrimp among 4 to 6 greased ramekins or serving shells or a shallow dish. Pour sauce over and sprinkle with Parmesan cheese. Place under the broiler, 4 inches from the heat, and cook until bubbly hot and lightly browned.

This is a favorite dish of the Formerly Fat Psychiatrist, so it has his highest recommendation. Though this is supposed to serve 4 at 210 calories each, many is the time it has served only 2 at our house.

MINCED CLAM SCALLOP

1 slice bacon, cut into 4 pieces
1 large onion, minced
1 cup sliced mushrooms
2 7-ounce cans minced clams
½ cup clam juice
½ teaspoon Worcestershire sauce
½ cup skimmed evaporated milk (page 3)
2 slices of toast, cubed
1 tablespoon grated cheese

Dry out the bacon in a heavy saucepan or skillet. Add the onion and mushrooms and fry for 5 minutes. Next add the clams, clam juice and Worcestershire sauce. Bring this to a boil and turn off the heat. Add the milk and toast cubes, gently mixing all together. If the mixture appears to be too dry, add some more clam juice. Turn into a shallow baking dish or into individual ramekins. Sprinkle the cheese on top and bake for 15 minutes in a 400° oven.

This will serve 6 at 120 calories per portion.

STUFFED CLAMS ORIENTALE

3 7-ounce cans minced clams
1 cup clam juice
1 tablespoon cornstarch
1 tablespoon soy sauce
¼ cup minced scallions
1 cup tiny green peas, cooked or canned
¼ cup chopped water chestnuts

Drain the clams and measure the juice; add enough bottled clam juice to make 1 cup. Mix together the cornstarch, soy sauce and clam juice. Cook over low heat, stirring constantly until thickened. Stir in the scallions, peas, water chestnuts and clams. Heat thoroughly and divide among 8 shells or ramekins. Bake in a 425° oven for 10 minutes.

Each shell has 60 calories.

CLAM BURGERS

1 14-ounce can minced clams	2 cups crushed Puffed Rice
1 medium onion, chopped	fresh pepper to taste
¼ teaspoon Worcestershire sauce	1 egg, slightly beaten
	1 slice bacon

Drain the clams well, but reserve the broth. Mix the clams, onion, Worcestershire sauce, crushed Puffed Rice and pepper together, adding enough broth to moisten. Add the egg and blend in well. Warm the skillet and put in half a slice of bacon. Drop the clam mixture by the heaping tablespoonful into the pan. If needed, you can add the other half of the bacon for frying the burgers. You will get 20 to 30 burgers, depending upon what kind of a heaper you are. The entire batch, however, contains 470 calories. They are very good, but do not expect them to taste like other burgers, for they are as related as ham is to a hamburger. Try them with one of the seafood dressings or chili sauce.

CLAM AND EGGPLANT CASSEROLE

2 cups cubed eggplant	seasoned salt
1 tablespoon butter	2 tablespoons minced green pepper
½ cup bread crumbs	1 large onion, grated
2 10-ounce cans minced clams	1 tablespoon flour

Wash and cube the unpeeled eggplant and parboil for 5 minutes. Lightly grease a casserole with some of the butter. Mix the remainder of the butter with 2 tablespoons of bread crumbs to be used later for a topping. Alternate layers in the casserole beginning with the eggplant, then the clams, seasoned salt, green pepper, onion and the remaining bread crumbs; repeat. Sprinkle each layer with a little flour. Top with buttered bread crumbs and bake for 30 minutes at 325°.

This will serve 4 hearty portions, each one having 150 calories. I must confess that there is only one member of my family who likes this dish. However, since he is the dieter, I feel obliged to include it in this collection.

CRAB MEAT CASSEROLE

1 large green pepper	¼ cup dietetic mayonnaise
2 pimientos	2 eggs
½ teaspoon salt	¼ cup dry sherry
¾ teaspoon pepper	2½ pounds fresh crab
1¼ tablespoons dry	meat
mustard	paprika

Seed and dice the green pepper; dice the pimientos. Mix the two together with the salt, pepper, mustard, dietetic mayonnaise, eggs and sherry, stirring until the mixture is very well blended. Preheat the oven to 350°; butter a 2-quart casserole. Very carefully fold the crab meat into the pepper mixture, and turn into the prepared casserole. Coat the top of the crab meat mixture with a very thin layer of mayonnaise; dust with paprika and bake for 20 minutes, or until the crab meat is done and the vegetables are tender.

Serve hot to 6 (each portion: 180 calories).

CRAB SOUFFLÉ

2 tablespoons powdered flour
2 tablespoons water
1 cup skimmed evaporated milk (page 3)
1 teaspoon Worcestershire sauce
½ teaspoon minced parsley
3 eggs, separated
1 cup flaked crab meat
2 tablespoons bread crumbs
½ tablespoon melted butter

Make a cream sauce as follows: Dissolve powdered flour in water. Add this to skimmed evaporated milk and stir over medium heat until thickened, seasoning with salt and pepper.

Add Worcestershire sauce, parsley, beaten egg yolks and crab meat to the cream sauce and cool. Pour into a casserole. Beat the egg whites and fold into the crab mixture. Toss the bread crumbs with the melted butter and sprinkle on top. Bake at 350° for 35 to 40 minutes.

This is a great luncheon dish for 4 (if you want to fuss for lunch), and the calorie count is only 190 per serving. It is also good as a first course for company, in which case you could share it with 6.

POACHED SCALLOPS

1½ pounds sea scallops
1 cup water
½ cup white wine
3 tablespoons lemon juice
1 small onion
2 parsley sprigs
salt and pepper
small piece of bay leaf
celery salt

Wash the scallops and put them in a shallow saucepan with boiling water and wine. Add the remaining ingredients and poach until just done (about 4 or 5 minutes). Drain the scallops and chill them. Before serving, you can toss with parsley dressing, cucumber sauce or low-calorie mayonnaise sprinkled with curry and capers. If you prefer, each of these dressings can be served separately.

Each of 4 portions has 171 calories.

MUSHROOM AND SEAFOOD CASEROLE

1 tablespoon butter
1 pound fresh mushrooms
1 green pepper, chopped
2 medium onions, sliced thin
4 cups cooked shellfish: lobster, crab, clams, shrimp (1 of each or any combination)
1 cup cooked rice
½ cup skimmed evaporated milk (page 3)
½ teaspoon thyme
½ teaspoon marjoram
salt
paprika
3 tablespoons chili sauce

In a heated pan, melt the butter and slowly cook the mushrooms, green pepper and onion. They should be cooked until they are soft but not brown. It is a good idea to cover them for the first few minutes of cooking. Combine these ingredients with the shellfish and warm thoroughly.

Grease a casserole and arrange the rice on the bottom and seafood mixture next. Mix the milk, herbs, salt, paprika and chili sauce, blending well. Pour the liquid over the seafood and bake at 375° for 20 minutes.

This will do for 4 hearty portions at 231 calories each. Since lobster has the highest caloric value, I only use 1 cup of it. If you want to keep the calorie content very low because your hearty dieter might eat the entire serving for 4 (I've had this happen to me quite a number of times, especially when I've allowed the dieter to serve himself), then use clams and crab meat.

QUICK SEAFOOD SALAD

1 can minced clams
1 can crab meat or lobster
1 tablespoon minced green pepper
½ teaspoon capers
1 tablespoon minced onion
2 tablespoons chopped celery
½ teaspoon curry powder
salt and pepper
1 tablespoon mayonnaise or salad dressing
1 can tiny shrimp

All the cans of shellfish should be the small size (about 6 ounces each). Drain the clams and save the liquid; you might need it for another recipe such as the baked mussels on page 27. Shred the crab or lobster meat and mix all of the ingredients, *except* the shrimp. (If you enjoy low-calorie mayonnaise, then you can use more than 1 tablespoon, but if you are using the regular kind, stick to the recipe.) When all the ingredients have been mixed well, add the shrimp and toss lightly so that they don't get crushed. If you prefer a moist salad, use some of the clam liquor. The entire recipe contains 375 calories. It can be served as an appetizer for 4, a spread for cocktails and/or a luncheon for 2.

I have found it very helpful to keep cans of seafood in the refrigerator so that I can whip up an emergency dish in a hurry.

SAUCE FOR SHELLFISH

½ cup thick buttermilk
1 tablespoon mayonnaise
freshly ground pepper
2 teaspoons capers

½ teaspoon curry powder
1 tablespoon freshly
chopped parsley

Mix and blend all ingredients well, chill and serve with cold cooked mussels or shrimp or use for a cold seafood salad. In the recipe, the mayonnaise is not low-calorie; therefore, if you have a low-calorie mayonnaise that you like, you can safely use more than 1 tablespoon.

This entire recipe contains 130 calories.

FISH

COURT BOUILLON

This is used to poach fish. You then serve the fish with your favorite dressing.

1 quart water
⅓ cup vinegar
1 carrot
1 tablespoon salt

1 onion with
  2 cloves stuck into it
1 stalk celery
2 lemon slices

Combine the above ingredients and cook 10 minutes. This can be prepared beforehand and left in the refrigerator for a few days. When you simmer fish in court bouillon, do not overcook it. As soon as the fish begins to flake, it is finished. Remove it carefully and serve.

POACHED HALIBUT, NEAR-EAST

2 pounds halibut
1 teaspoon ground
  turmeric
freshly ground pepper to
  taste
3 cups buttermilk

1 tablespoon lemon juice
1 teaspoon salt
1 tablespoon cumin seed
3 tablespoons chopped
  green pepper
1 tablespoon butter

Wash and dry the fish and cut it into 6 portions. Rub the fish with the turmeric and pepper. Warm the buttermilk and gently poach the fish for 6 minutes. Remove the fish and place in a baking dish in a warm oven. Let the buttermilk simmer until you have about 2 cups of liquid left, then add the lemon juice. Salt the fish, pour the liquid over it and add the cumin and green pepper. Return to a hot oven for 10 minutes. Brown the butter in a hot pan and pour it over the fish just before serving.

This is a hearty fish and will serve 6 at 192 calories per portion.

HALIBUT MIMI

Use eastern halibut cut into steaks, allowing 6 ounces per person. This sauce serves 6:

1 7-ounce can tomato
  sauce
2 tablespoons olive oil
½ green pepper, minced
juice of 1 lemon

¾ tomato sauce can of
  water (or white wine)
2 garlic cloves, crushed
6 sprigs torn parsley
salt and pepper to taste

Mix all the ingredients and boil them for 20 minutes. Add the fish, cover and simmer for 20 minutes. Refrigerate *overnight*.

Remove the dish from the refrigerator the following day, preheat the oven to 400° and heat thoroughly, uncovered. Serve and enjoy at 225 calories per portion. This is a great company dish, especially if you use white wine instead of water.

Incidentally, this basic sauce is good for veal and vegetables, BUT you must allow them to marinate a day before serving.

TUNA SCALLOP

2 7-ounce cans drained tuna
2 tablespoons oil from the tuna
2 tablespoons flour
½ teaspoon salt
¼ teaspoon pepper
½ cup diced celery
¼ teaspoon thyme
1 cup skimmed milk
1 cup mushrooms
1 cup cooked string beans, cut
½ cup cooked carrots, diced

Flake the tuna fish and set it aside. Heat the oil from the tuna and blend in the flour and seasonings. Add the milk gradually and cook until thickened. Mix this with the tuna fish and the vegetables. Place in a slightly greased casserole and bake at 350° for 30 minutes.

This meal-in-a-dish is excellent for lunch. The recipe will serve 6 at 208 calories per portion.

CHABLIS FLOUNDER

¼ cup Chablis
2 tablespoons lemon juice
1 bay leaf
¼ teaspoon salt
6 peppercorns
8 large onion slices
8 flounder fillets (approximately 4 ounces per fillet)
1 tablespoon butter
1 tablespoon flour
2 egg yolks beaten with 2 tablespoons water

First set the oven for 350°. In an 8-ounce jar, mix the wine, lemon juice, bay leaf, salt and peppercorns. Whisk them around a few times with a fork or wire whisk. Place the onion slices in a shallow baking dish. On each onion slice place a flounder fillet. Pour the contents of the jar over the fish, then cover with tinfoil. Bake at 350° for 15 minutes.

Remove the fillets, but try to keep them warm. Strain the sauce. You will need a cup of liquid, so if you find that you are short, add water. Melt the butter and slowly blend in the flour; then add both to the sauce and simmer slowly until it begins to thicken. At this point, you may add the beaten egg yolks and cook the sauce for another minute. Place the fillets in the baking dish once again and pour the sauce over them. Return the fish to a 400° oven for 5 minutes.

Four of you can have a very ample main dish for only 240 calories each (and if you want to know what to do with those 2 egg whites, look at pages 91 and 93.

FLOUNDER PARMESAN

2 pounds flounder fillet
6 tablespoons grated Parmesan cheese
1 tablespoon grated onion
1 cup buttermilk
1 tablespoon lemon juice
1½ teaspoons salt
dash of red hot sauce
paprika
chopped fresh parsley

Arrange the fish in a single layer in a baking dish. Mix all the other ingredients, *except* the parsley and the paprika. Spread the mixture over the fish and sprinkle with paprika. Bake for 25 minutes at 350°. Just before serving, sprinkle with the freshly chopped parsley.

This tempting fish recipe will serve 6 at 160 calories each.

LENORE'S BROILED FILLETS

Allow 2 fillets of sole for each portion. This sauce is enough for one portion:

4 tablespoons tomato juice or 2 tablespoons lemon juice

2 tablespoons cottage cheese

onion salt, seasoned salt or your favorite spices to taste

paprika

Wash and dry the fillets. Place juice in a baking pan and put the fillets on top. Mix the spices with the cheese and spread over the fillets. Sprinkle with paprika and broil under medium heat for about 10 minutes. There is no need to turn. The fish is ready when the top is crusty. This is a wonderfully easy dish and extremely good eating. Best of all, it is only 175 calories per portion.

SALMON STEAKS WITH WINE SAUCE

2 pounds fresh salmon steaks

salt and pepper to taste

3 ounces sherry

2 cloves garlic, chopped

1 teaspoon olive oil for each steak

juice of 2 lemons

Preheat the oven to 400°. Grease a deep baking pan and put the salmon steaks in it. Sprinkle with salt and pepper. Combine remaining ingredients and pour over fish. Bake until tender, about half an hour, but do not overcook.

If necessary, baste with more lemon juice.

Two pounds of salmon yield about 8 steaks; each steak has 253 calories.

FISH IN CHEESE SAUCE

1 tablespoon butter

1 tablespoon flour

¾ cup skimmed milk

1 teaspoon salt

¼ teaspoon pepper

½ cup grated Cheddar cheese

2 pounds fish fillets

1 tablespoon chives

fresh parsley

Melt the butter in a saucepan (one that will be large enough to accommodate the milk and cheese). Add the flour and stir into the melted butter until they are well blended. Slowly add the

milk, stirring continuously; add the salt and pepper and when the sauce begins to thicken, add
the cheese. Keep stirring until the cheese melts.
Arrange the fish in a shallow baking dish and
pour the sauce over the fish. Sprinkle the chives
on top. Bake at 375° for about 30 minutes or
until the top is browned and the fish flakes
easily. Garnish with parsley.

This will serve 4 heartily at 259 calories each.

EASY BAKED FILLETS

Cream of mushroom soup recipe (page 13), with
changes noted below

butter   2 pounds fish fillets
                    lemon juice

Follow the soup recipe, but use only 2 cups of
water to 4 bouillon cubes and increase the milk
by ½ cup. This will increase the basic calorie
count for fish (about 160) by another 60 calories.

Preheat the oven to 350°. Lightly grease a
shallow baking dish with butter and place the
fillets in it. Sprinkle lemon juice on the fillets.
Pour the cream of mushroom soup over this, and
bake uncovered for about 35 minutes, until the
fish flakes easily. Incidentally, this recipe serves 4.

Meat

GRAVY FOR MEAT

2 cups water
1 clove garlic, split
5 meat-flavored bouillon cubes
½ cup sliced mushrooms (optional)

2 tablespoons powdered flour
½ cup tomato sauce
1 tablespoon salad mustard
salt and pepper to taste

Bring the water to a boil with the garlic; add the bouillon and mushrooms. Simmer for 10 minutes, if you use mushrooms. If not, as soon as the bouillon has dissolved, you can add the flour slowly, then the tomato sauce, mustard, salt and pepper. Remove the garlic before serving.

This makes about 2½ cups of gravy. It is useful for leftover sliced beef or to disguise a new meat recipe that didn't turn out too well. There are 110 calories in the 2½ cups.

If you wish a gravy for chicken or veal, use chicken bouillon cubes. For fish you might try clam broth.

BARBECUED RIBS OF BEEF

3 pounds rib bones or
   short ribs
2 teaspoons salt
¼ teaspoon pepper
1 teaspoon paprika
1 teaspoon dry mustard
1 tablespoon Worcester-
   shire sauce

½ cup catsup
½ cup water
¼ cup cider vinegar
½ cup minced onions
1 clove garlic, minced
sugar substitute equal to
   1 tablespoon sugar

Use the top of the roast beef bones. Have them cut in 2-inch pieces and remove all visible fat. Brown the ribs in a heated casserole or Dutch oven; pour off the fat. Combine all the remaining ingredients and add to the ribs. Cover and bake in a 350° oven for 2 hours. Remove the cover for the last half hour.

This is a wonderful dish in many ways. It can be cooked the day before it is served; it can be used for hors d'oeuvres or as a main dish—and best of all is its taste!

If you serve 6, each portion will have 200 calories—but remember: strip the beef of all fat!

SHORT RIBS OF BEEF

3 pounds short ribs
seasoned salt and pepper
   to taste
¼ teaspoon chili powder
2 teaspoons monosodium
   glutamate
1 pound can stewed
   tomatoes

⅓ cup snipped celery
   leaves
¼ cup chopped green
   pepper
1 tablespoon lemon juice
lemon slices for garnish-
   ing

Try to get the leanest ribs possible. Have the butcher trim them and then you trim them too. Wipe clean and season with salt, pepper, chili powder and monosodium glutamate. Sear in a Dutch oven or similar pot. Add the tomatoes, celery leaves and green pepper, and simmer for 2 to 2½ hours, until tender. Stir in the lemon juice. Simmer another 10 minutes and serve garnished with the lemon slices. In serving this to the dieter, the ribs should be lifted out of the sauce and allowed to drain for a few seconds before reaching the plate since whatever fat did remain on the ribs will be in the sauce.

Four can eat away happily for 350 calories each.

POT ROAST BAKED IN RED WINE

2 pounds stewing beef, very lean, cut in cubes
salt and pepper to taste
½ teaspoon thyme
1 bay leaf
½ cup dry red table wine
12 small white onions
1 tablespoon capers
1 teaspoon Worcestershire sauce
½ cup sliced mushrooms (optional)
2 tablespoons minced parsley

A good cut for this dish is round steak.

Wipe the meat dry and season with salt, pepper and thyme. Heat a heavy casserole and sear the beef so that all sides are brown. Add the rest of the ingredients, *except* the parsley, cover and bake until tender. In a 350° oven, this should take about 1½ hours. Check it from time to time; you may have to add more water and a little (1 tablespoon) wine. When the beef is tender, sprinkle it with parsley.

At 353 calories each, you have 6 ample portions and you may even have some left over for lunch the following day.

P.S. This is even good enough for the boss when he comes for dinner. It can easily be prepared the night before or early in the morning.

SAUERKRAUT BEEF

3 pounds lean beef for boiling
3 onions
1½ teaspoons salt
¼ teaspoon pepper
1 teaspoon paprika
1½ pounds sauerkraut
1 bay leaf
1 cup boiling water

Trim the fat and cut the beef in 2-inch cubes; braise with the onions. Sprinkle with salt, pepper and paprika. Cover and cook over low heat for 30 minutes. Stir in the sauerkraut. Cook for 10 minutes. Add the bay leaf and water. Cover and cook an additional 1½ hours. Remove the bay leaf.

This is a real lazy-day meal-in-a-dish. You can fix it in the morning while you are tidying up the house and then take the day off and go shopping. Serve this dish to 8 with a little horseradish on the side and each portion will come to 285 calories.

BEEF STROGANOFF

1 tablespoon sour cream
½ cup buttermilk
½ pound mushrooms
½ tablespoon butter
2 pounds tender beef, pounded and cut in strips 2 by 2½ inches

1 can onion soup
¼ cup dry white wine
½ teaspoon freshly ground pepper
1 tablespoon powdered flour
paprika

Blend the sour cream and buttermilk and set aside. Slice the mushrooms, caps and stems, very thin. Warm the skillet, put in the butter and sauté the mushrooms for 3 to 4 minutes. (If the mushrooms are canned, there is no need to sauté them.) Remove the mushrooms and sauté the meat, browning it quickly on both sides. Heat the soup and add the wine; turn the flame up high for 1 minute. Return the mushrooms to the skillet with the meat, add the soup and pepper, and simmer until tender. Remove the meat, add the flour and cook the sauce until thickened and somewhat reduced. Return the meat to the skillet.

Warm the mixture when you are ready to

serve it and add the buttermilk and sour cream mixture. Sprinkle with paprika and heat thoroughly, but try not to boil it. (I hope you're more successful at it than I am!)

This recipe will serve 6 at 308 calories each. I realize this appears rather high, but you must remember that the beef alone is 230 calories, so for another 78 calories, you have a change-of-pace food that is still within the limits of the dieter.

SUKIYAKI

2 pounds sirloin or fillet or round steak
½ cup soy sauce
½ cup beef broth
¼ cup beer
sugar substitute equal to 3 tablespoons sugar
¼ teaspoon pepper
1 cup sliced scallions
¾ teaspoon monosodium glutamate
2 tablespoons oil
2 cups sliced onions
1 cup sliced celery
1 cup sliced bamboo shoots
1 cup sliced mushrooms

Cut the meat cross-grain in paper-thin slices. (Slightly frozen meat is easier to slice thin.) Combine the soy sauce, broth, beer, sugar substitute, pepper and monosodium glutamate. Heat the oil in a skillet; brown the steak in it. Push to one side of the pan and pour ½ cup of the soy sauce mixture over it. Add the onions, celery, bamboo shoots and mushrooms; sauté for 3 minutes. Pour remaining soy sauce mixture into the pan and add the scallions; cook for 3 minutes. NOTE: Chicken or pork may be substituted for the beef.

Serve a clear soup first and perhaps a few tablespoons of boiled rice with the Sukiyaki; a leafy salad and sherbet round out the dinner. This meal will serve 6 at 350 calories each.

MEAT BALL CASSEROLE

4 teaspoons butter
1 cup chopped onion
1 clove garlic, minced or crushed
4 tablespoons bread crumbs
1 egg, beaten
3 pounds ground round steak

2 teaspoons salt
½ teaspoon freshly ground pepper
½ teaspoon thyme
1 pound sliced mushrooms
6 ounces dry white wine
½ cup skimmed evaporated milk (page 3)

1 cup beef bouillon

Melt 2 teaspoons of butter in a skillet and sauté the onion until it is golden brown. Mix the garlic and the bread crumbs and toss with the onions in the hot skillet for a few minutes. Remove these ingredients from the skillet. Mix the egg into the meat with salt, pepper and thyme; blend thoroughly with the crumb and onion mixture. You should knead the meat with your fingers for 5 minutes. Shape it into balls (about 2 inches in diameter). Brown them in the skillet and then transfer them to a casserole. Sauté the mushrooms in the skillet from which you just removed the meat balls. Mix the wine, milk and bouillon together and pour over the meat balls. Bake in a covered casserole for 30 minutes at 350°. Uncover the casserole and bake for another 10 minutes. (You can serve this on the following day, if you like.) There are 334 calories in each of 8 portions.

If you make these meat balls smaller, you will have an excellent dish for hors d'oeuvres.

STUFFED PEPPERS

2 onions, diced
1 clove garlic, split
1 tablespoon butter
1 pound lean chopped beef
1 teaspoon salt
4 or 5 drops Worcestershire sauce

1 egg
1 cup cooked sliced mushrooms (optional)
6 tablespoons cooked rice
6 green peppers
1 can tomatoes (1½ cups)

Sauté the onion and garlic in butter over a low fire until the onion becomes transparent. Discard the garlic (optional, but crush it if you prefer and keep it), and mix the onions with the meat, salt, Worcestershire sauce, egg, mushrooms and rice in the frying pan and toss lightly over a high flame until the meat loses its raw look. Take the tops off the peppers, clean them out and stuff them with the meat mixture. Place the tomatoes in a pan that will hold all the peppers. The peppers should be packed in rather tightly so that they will not fall over. Cover the pot and simmer about 20 minutes, at which time the peppers should be tender. Serve with a topping of the tomato sauce.

Each stuffed pepper has 181 calories.

SWEETBREADS

When prepared properly, sweetbreads make an excellent main dish for the dieter. There are only 100 calories in 4 ounces. This is an expensive cut of meat, but it cannot be eaten in the same quantity as other meats. Therefore, when serving sweetbreads, the cook has an opportunity to offer a hearty soup or dessert with the meal without providing too many calories.

Another interesting feature of sweetbreads is that they can be prepared with utmost simplicity.

Pre-cooked Sweetbreads

Use calf or lamb sweetbreads, allowing ½ to 1 pair per person. Cover with cold water, let stand for 30 minutes and then drain. Cover with boiling water, adding 1 teaspoon salt and 1 tablespoon vinegar for each quart of water. Cool enough to handle; remove all membrane. You can prepare sweetbreads 24 hours before you intend to use them.

Broiled Sweetbreads

Follow the directions for Pre-cooked Sweet-breads. Halve crosswise; sprinkle with salt and pepper. Brush with melted butter or margarine. Place on broiler rack with the top of the food 3 inches below flame. Broil about 10 minutes, turning once.

Braised Sweetbreads

Use calf or lamb sweetbreads, allowing ½ to 1 pair per person. Cover with cold water, let stand 30 minutes and then drain. Remove all membrane. Dip sweetbreads in seasoned flour; sauté in small amount of fat or salad oil, turning to brown on all sides. Cover; cook slowly for 20 minutes. If desired, blend together a little flour and white dry wine (2 to 3 tablespoons); add to drippings in pan in which sweetbreads were cooked. Cook the sauce, stirring constantly, until thickened. Serve on sweetbreads.

There are 200 calories in each pair of sweetbreads.

SWEETBREADS WITH CHESTNUTS AND MUSHROOMS

6 pairs sweetbreads	3 tablespoons Madeira
1 tablespoon vinegar	¾ cup chicken bouillon
2 teaspoons salt	¼ teaspoon freshly
2 tablespoons butter	ground black pepper
1 cup chopped onion	¼ cup diced ham
¾ cup grated carrot	1 cup sliced mushrooms
½ cup chopped celery	1 cup coarsely chopped
¼ cup dry white wine	cooked chestnuts

Soak the sweetbreads in cold water for 2 hours in the refrigerator. Drain and cover with fresh water. Add the vinegar and salt. Bring to a boil and cook 5 minutes. Drain and remove the membranes. Place a weight on the sweetbreads (a breadboard or a plate) and chill. Melt 1 tablespoon butter in a preheated skillet; sauté the onion, carrot and celery, covered, for 10 minutes. Add the white wine and Madeira. Arrange the sweetbreads in the skillet and add enough of the bouillon to half-cover them. Season with the pepper, then cover them and bake at 350° for 30 minutes.

Melt the remaining 1 tablespoon butter in another skillet and sauté the ham, mushrooms and chestnuts for 5 minutes. If you find that these ingredients are sticking to the skillet, you can put a cover on it and steam them. Add this mixture to the sweetbreads, then check for seasoning and serve.

This recipe serves 6 and contains 293 calories per portion.

LIVER MARSALA

1 pound liver, sliced about ¼-inch thick	1 teaspoon salt
	¼ teaspoon white pepper
2 tablespoons powdered flour	1 tablespoon margarine
	3 ounces Marsala
2 tablespoons lemon juice	

Wipe the liver dry and remove any tough fibers. Mix flour, salt and pepper and spread out on a board. Dust the liver lightly with this mixture. Heat a coated pan, adding half the margarine to start with, and quickly brown the liver on both sides (about 3 minutes). Set the liver aside in a shallow bake-and-serve pan. When all the pieces are fried, add the wine and lemon juice to the pan, scrape around the pan and simmer for 2 minutes. Pour this sauce over the liver and heat in the oven (400°) for about 3 to 5 minutes.

This will serve 4 people at 280 calories each and is particularly popular with those people who claim to be liver haters.

LIVER DIVINE

1½ pounds calves liver
1 tablespoon butter
1½ cups thinly sliced onion
1 teaspoon salt
¼ teaspoon freshly ground black pepper
¼ cup dry white wine
2 tablespoons minced parsley

Cut the liver in paper-thin slices and then into strips about 1 inch by 2 inches.

Melt the butter in a preheated skillet; add the onion slices. Cover and cook the onions over very low heat 15 minutes, or until lightly browned and soft. Add the liver, and cook over high heat for 3 minutes, stirring almost constantly. Season with salt and pepper. Transfer to a hot platter. Stir the wine and parsley into the skillet; bring to a boil and pour over the liver.

This will give you 4 servings at 242 calories each.

VEAL IN VERMOUTH SAUCE

1½ pounds veal scaloppine
2 tablespoons flour
1¼ teaspoons salt
¼ teaspoon white pepper
2 tablespoons butter
¼ cup dry vermouth
½ cup skimmed evaporated milk (page 3)

You should have about 12 pieces of veal. Be sure the veal is cut thin, then pounded. Dip the pieces lightly in a mixture of flour, salt and pepper. Melt the butter in a skillet; brown the veal in it over high heat. Add the vermouth, bring to a boil and cook a few seconds. Add the skimmed milk, shaking the pan until the mixture boils; then cook over low heat for 5 minutes, turning the veal once.

This will serve 4, at 380 calories each. It's even good enough for company.

COMPANY VEAL

1 slice bacon
3 pounds boneless veal, cut in 1½-inch cubes
12 small white onions
3 carrots, sliced
1½ teaspoons salt
½ teaspoon white pepper
1 clove garlic, minced
3 tablespoons powdered flour
½ cup dry red wine
2 teaspoons finely chopped bay leaves
¼ teaspoon thyme
½ pound mushrooms, sliced and sautéed
2 tablespoons minced parsley

Divide the bacon into 4 pieces and brown it in a large skillet. As the fat begins to accumulate, brown the veal, onions and carrots. Sprinkle with the salt, pepper, garlic and flour; add the wine, bay leaves and thyme. Cover and cook over low heat for 1¼ hours, or until the veal is tender. Skim off the fat. Add the mushrooms and parsley. Cook 5 minutes longer. Taste for seasoning.

This is an excellent cook-ahead company dish, especially good for serving buffet style. You can get 8 portions from this recipe with a calorie count of 350 per portion.

PORK CHOPS SUPREME

Sear pork chops on both sides. Season with salt and pepper. Place in a baking dish, and place on each chop 1 slice of raw onion, 1 ring of green pepper and 1 heaping tablespoon boiled rice. Empty a small can of tomatoes over all. Cover closely and bake in a moderate oven for 2 hours. Add a little water if needed.

This is a great recipe for someone who doesn't have the time to watch over fried or broiled pork chops. The average rib chop contains 310 calories; this recipe will increase that amount by 25 calories.

BOILED PICKLED TONGUE

3 to 5 pound pickled   1 onion
   tongue   2 cloves garlic
                    2 bay leaves

Wash the tongue. Combine with onion, garlic and bay leaves in a deep kettle. Cover with water. Bring to a boil and cook over medium heat for 3½ hours or until tender. If necessary, add boiling water as the liquid cooks out. Let the tongue cool in the stock; then remove the root and the skin. Reserve 2 cups of stock if you want to make a sauce.

This recipe serves 6 to 8. When serving 6 there will be 200 calories per portion. Boiled tongue is good to have on hand; slice it thin and use as emergency food between meals.

If mustard is not enough of a sauce, you can make a simple Orange and Raisin Sauce to accompany the tongue. This will add 54 calories per portion.

ORANGE AND RAISIN SAUCE

2 tablespoons seedless   4 ounces orange juice
   raisins   2 ounces port wine
1½ cups stock   sugar substitute equal to
2 chicken bouillon cubes   ¼ cup sugar
1 tablespoon butter   ⅛ teaspoon ground cloves
1 tablespoon powdered
   flour

Simmer the raisins in the stock for 5 minutes. (Use meat, fish or chicken stock depending on what the sauce accompanies.) Dissolve the bouillon cubes in the stock, maintaining the 1½ cups. Melt the butter in a preheated saucepan and gradually add the flour, stirring continuously. Slowly add the orange juice, mixing steadily. Combine this with the bouillon and add the wine, sugar substitute and cloves. Simmer for 5 minutes.

You could try this sauce with boiled chicken or broiled fish fillets as well as tongue.

This recipe makes 2 cups of sauce, with a total of 324 calories.

Chicken

STUFFED BROILERS

3 small broilers, split
3 teaspoons salt
¾ teaspoon freshly
  ground black pepper
2 tablespoons butter
1 cup chopped onion
3 cups sliced mushrooms
½ cup chopped celery and
  leaves

¾ pound chicken livers,
  chopped
¼ teaspoon thyme
2 tablespoons minced
  parsley
6 tablespoons cooked rice
¼ cup orange juice
¼ cup dry sherry

Wash and dry the chicken halves; season with 2 teaspoons salt and ½ teaspoon pepper.

For the stuffing, melt 1 tablespoon of butter in a skillet; sauté the onion, mushrooms and celery 5 minutes. Mix in the livers and the remaining salt and pepper; sauté 5 minutes, stirring frequently. Mix in the thyme and parsley; taste for seasoning. Combine this mixture with the rice and orange juice.

Melt the remaining butter in a baking pan. Arrange the chicken halves in it, skin side up. Bake in a 350° oven for 20 minutes. Turn over, skin side down, and fill the cavities with the stuffing.

Pour the sherry over the stuffing and around the chicken. Bake 20 minutes longer, or until the chicken is tender.

This is as easy to make as plain broiled chicken, but it is practically a meal in itself. You can get 6 hearty portions for 429 calories each.

CHICKEN MARINARA

2 fryers, cut for frying
paprika
olive oil
2 onions, minced
2 cloves garlic, split
¼ cup fresh parsley
1 bay leaf
¼ teaspoon oregano
1½ cups canned plum
   tomatoes
4 anchovy fillets, mashed
1 tablespoon powdered
   flour

Dry the chicken, sprinkle with paprika and brown quickly on top of the stove in a coated pan or a heavy black frying pan that has been salted. Sauté the onion and garlic slowly in 2 teaspoons olive oil until they are transparent. Place all the remaining ingredients into a covered casserole, *except* the anchovies and flour. Cook on top of the stove about 40 minutes until tender. Remove the chicken, bay leaf and garlic. Add the mashed anchovies and flour, then simmer until thickened. Return the chicken to the pot and warm thoroughly. This dish is excellent when made the day before, or in the morning if it is to be served at dinner.

The recipe yields 6 good portions at only 250 calories each.

INSTANT CHICKEN ITALIENNE

4 onions, thinly sliced
2 tablespoons paprika
2 quartered broilers
salt and pepper to taste
½ cup dry white wine
1 garlic clove, crushed
2 pinches oregano
½ cup Marinara sauce

Place the onions in a heavy roaster on the top of the stove. Cover them with lots of paprika and turn the flame up rather high. Sauté the chicken (which has been cleaned, salted and peppered) on the onions, browning quickly on both sides. Mix the wine, garlic, oregano and Marinara sauce, pour over the chicken and cover. Place in the oven at 350° for 30 minutes; then remove the cover and cook until the chicken is tender and the sauce somewhat reduced. There should not be too much gravy because the dieter will be tempted to dunk bread into it; however, it should be quite moist. (*You* can always dunk a little bread before you bring the dish to the table.)

Six people can share this at 260 calories each.

CHILI CHICKEN

1 tablespoon butter
¼ cup chopped onion
1 cup minced green pepper
1 clove garlic, minced
1 tablespoon starch
1 cup double-strength chicken bouillon
1 4-ounce can tomato paste
½ cup sliced mushrooms
2 tablespoons fresh parsley
½ teaspoon sugar
½ teaspoon chili powder
3 pinches oregano
salt and black pepper to taste
1 4-ounce can water
3 cups cooked chicken, large chunks

This recipe calls for about 1½ pounds of chicken meat. It is a good way to serve boiled chicken, which you may have cooked just for the broth.

Melt the butter in a preheated skillet, then add the onion, green pepper and garlic. (If you intend to remove the garlic, don't mince it, merely split it in two.) Cook until the onion is soft and transparent; then blend in the starch. Remove from the fire, add the bouillon, tomato paste, mushrooms, parsley, sugar, chili powder, oregano, salt, pepper and water. Stir and blend well over heat until slightly thickened. Place the chicken chunks in a casserole and pour the sauce over it.

Bake for 30 minutes at 400°. This dish is for 5 hearty eaters and contains 273 calories per portion.

CHICKEN BREASTS IN SHERRY

4 whole chicken breasts with the wings attached
1 tablespoon melted butter
½ pound mushrooms (optional)
salt and pepper to taste
1 cup skimmed evaporated milk (page 3)
½ cup dry sherry

Remove the chicken skin (thereby reducing the caloric value), split breasts and brush with melted butter. Place the chicken under the broiler and brown quickly. Remove and season with salt and pepper. Combine the skimmed milk and sherry in a saucepan and bring to the simmering point. Arrange the chicken breasts in a casserole, pour the liquid over them, cover and bake at 300° for 40 minutes. Uncover, add the mushrooms and bake about 20 minutes longer. The sauce should be reduced and thickened. If not, remove the chicken and cook down the sauce, or thicken it with 1 tablespoon of powdered flour.

This is an excellent cook-ahead dish and it actually tastes better after it has marinated a day.

This recipe provides 6 generous portions at 211 calories each.

SUPER CHICKEN

2 fryers, cut up
1 tablespoon seasoned salt
¼ cup dry white wine
1 cup chicken bouillon
½ teaspoon instant onion
½ teaspoon curry powder
Sauce: 2 tablespoons powdered flour
¼ cup water
1 cup sliced canned mushrooms

Dry the chicken pieces and then dip them into the seasoned salt. Place in a baking dish. Mix the wine, bouillon, onion and curry and pour over the chicken. Cover with foil and bake at 350°

for 30 minutes. Uncover the dish and bake until tender (about another 30 minutes). Remove the juices and strain. Keep the chicken warm. Make the sauce by blending the flour and water with the juice over a low heat until thick. Add the mushrooms, warm them and spoon the sauce over the chicken. Serve.

This serves 6 people at 231 calories a serving —just 19 calories more than unadorned chicken.

TANGY OVEN-FRIED CHICKEN

2 broilers, cut up
1 teaspoon salt
1 clove garlic, minced
2 teaspoons curry powder
2 chicken bouillon cubes in ½ cup boiling water
½ teaspoon dry mustard in 1 tablespoon water
2 teaspoons Worcestershire sauce
1 teaspoon oregano
½ teaspoon paprika
2 to 3 dashes Tabasco

Salt the chicken and place skin side down in a shallow bake-and-serve dish. Mix all the other ingredients together and brush both sides of the chicken with the mixture. Bake in a 350° oven, turning and basting often, until tender. Just before serving, put into a 400° oven for 10 minutes (or broil for 5 minutes for a crisp chicken).

You can easily serve 6 at 220 calories each, allowing plenty of "leftover" calories for a special dessert.

HERBED CHICKEN BREAST

3 whole chicken breasts, split
¼ teaspoon each: basil, tarragon, thyme
salt and pepper to taste
1 tablespoon butter
juice of 1 lemon or lime

Dry the chicken breasts and sprinkle with the herbs, salt and pepper. Place them skin side down on tin foil 4 inches from the broiler. Melt the butter and blend in the lemon juice. Use half of this to brush on the chicken before broiling.

While broiling, baste with pan drippings. After
30 minutes, turn and baste with the remaining
lemon-butter sauce. Continue basting with pan
drippings as before until tender and crisp.

This will serve 4 at 265 calories each.

CHICKEN MUSHROOM SOUFFLÉ

1 tablespoon butter
1 tablespoon powdered
flour
½ cup mushroom liquor
½ cup skimmed evapo-
rated milk (page 3)
1 cup ground cooked
chicken

½ cup chopped mush-
rooms
1 teaspoon minced parsley
1 teaspoon finely cut
chives
paprika, salt and pepper
¼ teaspoon Worcester-
shire sauce

2 eggs, separated

Melt the butter in a preheated skillet, stir in the
flour, then slowly add the mushroom liquor and
the skimmed milk. Keep stirring this until it becomes thickened. Then add all other ingredients
except the eggs and simmer for 3 minutes. Remove the saucepan from the fire and let it cool
while you beat the egg yolks. Combine the egg
yolks with the milk mixture. Beat the egg whites
until they are stiff, but still moist. Fold the egg
whites into the milk-mushroom, etc., mixture.
Grease a small casserole and pour the soufflé ingredients into it. Bake at 350° for 35 minutes.
Serve immediately!

This will serve 4 at 198 calories per portion.

ALL-PURPOSE MOUSSE

I call this an all-purpose mousse because almost any food that can be chopped or flaked
could be substituted for the chicken. Of course,
you will have to adjust the caloric values accord-
ingly. If you use chicken, as I have done in this
recipe, 6 servings will have a caloric count of
103. If you use clams or crab meat, each portion

will amount to 53 calories. If you choose to make a mousse with lobster, each of 6 portions will amount to 70 calories. With salmon it will be 81 and with tuna fish (drain the oil), 75.

1 envelope unflavored gelatin
¼ cup dry white wine
2 egg yolks
¾ cup chicken bouillon
1 cup ground cooked chicken
2 tablespoons chopped parsley
1½ teaspoons lemon juice

1 teaspoon onion juice
salt, celery salt, paprika to taste
dash of cayenne pepper
1 tablespoon chopped fresh dill (or 1 teaspoon dried dill)
½ cup whipped skimmed evaporated milk (page 3)

Soften the gelatin in the wine. Put the egg yolks in a double boiler and beat them slightly. You must be careful with this because the yolks harden very rapidly, so begin to add the bouillon immediately and cook over hot water. Stir this combination constantly until the mixture thickens. Now remove it from the heat and add the softened gelatin, stirring until dissolved. Combine this with the rest of the ingredients (except the milk). Chill in a large bowl until it is almost jelled. At this point, fold in the whipped skimmed evaporated milk. Pour the mixture into a slightly greased mold and chill until firm.

If you are making a lobster or crab meat mousse, substitute clam juice.

CHICKEN AND MUSHROOM MOXIE

4 whole chicken breasts
2 tablespoons butter
1 small onion, chopped
salt to taste
¼ teaspoon pepper
½ cup chicken bouillon

1 pound mushrooms, thickly sliced
1 tablespoon cornstarch
1 cup skimmed evaporated milk (page 3)
¼ cup dry sherry

2 tablespoons toasted blanched almonds

Remove the skin and cube the chicken meat. Preheat a skillet and sauté the onion in 1 tablespoon butter until golden. Add the chicken, salt, pepper and chicken bouillon. Cover and simmer for 30 minutes, then add the mushrooms and simmer for 10 more minutes. Remove everything from the pan and reserve enough liquid so that you have 1 cup (if necessary, add water).

Melt 1 tablespoon of butter in the same skillet you used for the chicken, blend in the cornstarch and salt. Stir until smooth; gradually add the cup of liquid and the milk and bring to a boil. Reduce the heat and simmer for 5 minutes, stirring constantly. Return the chicken and mushrooms to the skillet, add the sherry and simmer uncovered for 5 minutes or until the chicken is thoroughly heated. Add the almonds just before serving.

My family enjoys this one very much. It has 333 calories for each of 6 servings.

MY MOTHER'S FRICASSEE

1 egg	salt and pepper
2 tablespoons water	1 large onion, minced
1 pound chopped beef	2 tablespoons paprika
2 tablespoons bread crumbs	½ pound chicken necks and gizzards
½ garlic clove, crushed	2 pounds chicken wings
½ pound chicken livers	

Beat the egg and the water with a fork and blend with the chopped beef, bread crumbs, garlic, salt and pepper. Knead this all together with your fingers for 5 minutes. Form into small cocktail-size meat balls. Warm a Dutch oven and cover the bottom with the onion and paprika. Brown the meat balls on the onions, turning frequently and then remove. Salt and pepper the gizzards and necks, place on top of the onions; then salt the wings and place them on the gizzards. Next come the meat balls. Pour ½ cup of water over all and simmer for 45 minutes. Cut the livers in half and add them to the pot; continue cooking until the livers are done. (The wings may be ready first, so remove them before they fall apart.) This is a great dish!

Six can share this pot of fricassee with a calorie count of 270 each.

Vegetables

BEAN SPROUTS

This vegetable is the dieter's best friend. It contains so few calories that you don't even have to bother to count them. It can also be the companion's greatest aid because it can be offered at any time and in unlimited quantities. With just a little experimenting, you can find numerous ways to flavor bean sprouts. They are only limited by your spice shelf.

Bean sprouts can be purchased canned (and they are cheap, too). But if you feel ambitious, you can easily grow them. It's fun to do, the kids will enjoy the experience and everyone will be sharing in the great challenge. As a matter of fact, this could be a job exclusively for the children.

Here's how to grow them. Bean sprouts come from mung peas which have to be purchased in an Oriental or Indian specialty shop. Each cup of dried peas will give you about 1 pound of sprouts. Wash the peas, cover them with water and let them stand overnight. Drain them well, then wrap them in a damp, clean kitchen towel and place the bundle in a colander. Keep it in a dark, warm place for three days, but remember to wet the towel each morning and night with warm water. Be sure to toss the sprouts around each time you dampen them so that they will not root into the towel. When sprouted, pick them over to remove the pea skins. Place them in a colander and scald the sprouts with boiling water. Rinse with cold water and drain. And there you are, a farmer in your own kitchen.

Basically, all that sprouts need for cooking is a thorough warming, quickly over a hot flame. They can be cooked with mushrooms, scallions, onions, celery, plain in a small quantity of olive oil with salt and pepper, or in butter with seasoned salt. There are endless combinations, so when you have hit upon a particularly good one be sure to write it down.

HAPPY EXPERIMENTING!

BEAN SPROUT-ONION SAUTÉ

½ tablespoon salad oil
1 medium onion, minced
    or 3 scallions, minced
1 pound can bean sprouts,
    well-drained
salt and pepper to taste
1 teaspoon Worcestershire sauce

Drop the oil in a preheated pan and sauté the onions or scallions until they are golden. Toss in the bean sprouts, salt, pepper and Worcestershire sauce. Heat quickly on a high flame, tossing the sprouts until they are hot. Serve immediately.

The calories in this recipe are all in the oil, so you can have as much of this as often as you like.

It's great as an emergency food.

BEETS CARAWAY

1 tablespoon sour cream	pepper
¼ cup buttermilk	½ pound beets, cooked,
1 tablespoon butter	sliced and drained
1 tablespoon lemon juice	½ teaspoon caraway seeds

Mix the sour cream and buttermilk with a fork or wire whisk and set aside. Melt the butter and add all the remaining ingredients. Toss and warm thoroughly, then add the milk and sour cream mixture. Continue warming but do not boil. This will serve 6 at 56 calories each.

BETTER BEETS

2 teaspoons butter	salt and pepper to taste
1 pinch ground basil	1 small can sliced beets,
2 teaspoons fresh parsley	very well drained

Melt the butter; add all the spices to the melted butter and blend well. Add the beets, cover and warm thoroughly. This has so few calories that they aren't even worth mentioning. Save this dish for a snack-time extra.

BEETS N'ORANGE JUICE

4 tablespoons orange juice	2 cups shredded beets
2 teaspoons lemon juice	1 tablespoon butter
1 teaspoon salt	2 teaspoons cornstarch

Combine the orange and lemon juices and salt in a saucepan. Bring them to a boil and add the beets. Cook fresh beets 10 minutes and canned about 4. Add the butter. Mix the cornstarch with 1 tablespoon of water or extra orange juice. Stir this into the beets until the sauce is thickened and clears.

This is a welcome change for a side dish and a good extra evening snack. If you want 4 portions out of this recipe, each one will have 81 calories.

BRUSSELS SPROUTS CARAWAY

½ cup chicken bouillon
2 cups frozen brussels
  sprouts
1 tablespoon butter

¼ teaspoon salt
⅛ teaspoon freshly
  ground pepper
1 teaspoon caraway seeds

Bring the bouillon to a boil and add the frozen sprouts. Cook them until they are tender and then drain well. Toss with butter, salt, pepper and caraway seeds. Serve immediately.

This is delightfully easy and tastes as though it's special. These 4 servings contain 50 calories each.

ORANGE-GLAZED CARROTS

12 carrots, quartered
  lengthwise
1 tablespoon butter
½ tablespoon brown sugar
sugar substitute equal to 1
  tablespoon sugar

¼ cup orange juice
3 whole cloves
¼ teaspoon salt
2 tablespoons minced
  parsley

Cook the carrots until they are tender but still quite firm. Drain them thoroughly. In a preheated skillet, melt the butter and blend in the brown sugar and the sugar substitute, orange juice, cloves and salt. Discard the cloves after a few minutes. Add the carrots and toss lightly over low heat until they are coated. Sprinkle with parsley and serve.

There are 62 calories in each of 4 portions.

BRAISED CARROTS

4 cups julienne carrots
⅓ cup water
1 tablespoon butter
1 teaspoon salt

sugar substitute equal to
  ½ cup sugar
1 tablespoon minced
  parsley
¼ teaspoon pepper

Put the carrots, water, butter, salt and sugar substitute in a saucepan, cover and cook until tender (about 15 minutes). Sprinkle with parsley and pepper. Then it's ready to serve.

This recipe will serve 6 at 43 calories each.

BAKED CARROTS

2 tablespoons butter
12 small size carrots,
  quartered
1 teaspoon salt
¼ cup minced onion
sugar substitute equal to 1
  tablespoon sugar
¼ teaspoon ginger
¼ cup skimmed evaporated milk (page 3)

Melt 1 tablespoon of butter and arrange the carrots over it. Sprinkle them with salt, onion, sugar substitute, ginger and milk. Cover and bake at 375° until tender (25 minutes). Remove the cover for 5 minutes and brush with the remaining butter.

This dish has a tangy quality that is refreshingly different.

Each of 6 servings is 61 calories.

EGGPLANT AND ANCHOVIES

2 small eggplants, split
3 teaspoons olive oil
2 cloves garlic
1 slice hard French bread,
  cubed
salt and pepper to taste
10 anchovy fillets, chopped
grated rind of 1 lemon
2 tablespoons lemon juice
½ pound mushrooms,
  sliced

Wash the eggplants, split them and scoop out the centers. Chop them coarsely. Using 1 teaspoon of oil, sauté the garlic and steam the chopped eggplant until tender. Remove the eggplant, but leave the garlic. Add another teaspoon of oil to the pan and sauté the bread. Add the remaining ingredients and mix thoroughly. Stuff this mixture into the eggplant shells and place them into a shallow baking dish with warm water covering the bottom of the dish. Bake at 375° for 35 minutes or until tender and well browned.

Use the remaining teaspoon of oil to dribble
over each half before baking.

Serve as the main dish for a luncheon or as a
side dish for dinner. Each half has 100 calories.

EGGPLANT STEW

1 tablespoon olive oil
1 cup chopped onion
1 green pepper in julienne
strips
1 medium eggplant,
peeled and cubed
1 cup chopped tomatoes
½ teaspoon salt
¼ teaspoon freshly
ground pepper
¼ teaspoon oregano

Prewarm the frying pan and add ½ tablespoon
of oil. Sauté the onions, covered for 2 minutes
and uncovered for 5. Add the remaining oil,
green pepper and eggplant; sauté this mixture,
stirring frequently. Combine the tomatoes, salt,
pepper and oregano with the ingredients in the
pan. Cook in a covered saucepan over low heat
for 30 minutes, adding a little boiling water if it
appears to be drying out.

This very filling side dish will serve 6 successfully at about 50 calories each.

EGGPLANT AND CALVES LIVER

2 small eggplants
¼ pound calves liver,
chopped
3 tomatoes, skinned and
chopped
3 small onions, chopped
1 cup chopped mush-
rooms
1 tablespoon oil
1 tablespoon flour
1 tablespoon tomato paste
2 tablespoons mixed
Italian herbs
½ teaspoon salt
pepper to taste
4 teaspoons grated
Parmesan cheese
4 teaspoons bread crumbs

Cut the eggplants in half and let them stand
in salted water for 30 minutes. Meanwhile broil
the liver until it is tender but not well done. Chop
the liver while it is still warm (it is easiest then).
When the 30 minutes are up, drain the eggplants
and simmer covered with the tomatoes until ten-

der. Remove from the pan. Sauté the onions and the mushrooms in oil for about 5 minutes. Scoop out the meat of the eggplant and chop. Mix the flour with the tomato paste; mix and thoroughly heat the tomatoes, tomato paste and flour mixture, onions and mushrooms, herbs, salt, pepper, eggplant and chopped liver. Fill each eggplant shell, sprinkle with cheese and bread crumbs (mix them together to get an even distribution).

Place under the broiler until the topping is slightly brown.

This recipe serves 4. Each shell has 144 calories. This dish can be served as an appetizer, for lunch or with cocktails.

EGGPLANT PARMEGIANA

1 large eggplant
1 tablespoon olive oil
6 tablespoons bread crumbs
3 tablespoons grated Parmesan cheese
½ teaspoon salt
¼ teaspoon pepper
½ teaspoon garlic powder
1 cup canned tomato sauce
3 thin slices Mozzarella cheese

Peel the eggplant and slice it in ¼-inch slices. Pour boiling water over the slices and soak them for 5 minutes. Then drain and pat dry. Heat a skillet and using 1 teaspoon of oil at a time, quickly brown the eggplant slices (try to beat my record of 2 teaspoons of oil for this one).

Mix the crumbs, Parmesan cheese, salt, pepper and garlic powder. In a shallow baking dish, arrange alternate layers of eggplant, crumb/spice mixture and tomato sauce. Cover the final layer with Mozzarella cheese and bake at 325° for 25 minutes.

You can add a few tablespoons of Marinara sauce to the tomato sauce if you enjoy spicy food.

This recipe serves 6 people at 105 calories

each; combine it with a hearty salad and dessert
and you will have an elegant dinner.

GREEN BEANS AND MUSHROOMS AMANDINE

1 pound green beans
1 tablespoon butter
¼ cup chopped onions
½ pound sliced mush-
rooms
¾ teaspoon salt
2 dashes pepper

2 tablespoons sliced
toasted almonds
1 teaspoon heavy sweet
cream mixed with 4
tablespoons skimmed
evaporated milk (page
3)

Cook and drain the green beans, then return
them to the saucepan. Preheat a frying pan and
melt the butter. Sauté the onions for 5 minutes;
add the mushrooms and sauté them for 5 minutes.
Mix in the salt, pepper and almonds and cook for
1 minute, stirring all the time. Add the cream-
milk mixture to the beans and bring almost to a
boil. Place the beans in a serving dish with the
mushroom mixture on top.

This is a very good side dish for 6 but would
serve 3 or 4 for a main course at lunch. Count on
55 calories for each as a side dish.

HOT KRAUT

Count on ½ pound for each person because
this is good!

To steam the sauerkraut, place ½ cup of water
in a heavy saucepan, put a wire or mesh grill over
the water and add 2 pounds of sauerkraut. Mix
into the sauerkraut 2 slices of bacon cut in half,
1 large frankfurter (a special) cut into small
pieces and any leftover ham (a small amount).
Steam for 1 hour.

CAUTION: Do not let the dieter see anything but
the sauerkraut! The meats are for flavoring *only*
(or for you to eat in the kitchen while he's not

looking). Remove all the meats; sprinkle the sauerkraut liberally with kimmel seeds and serve.

This is a great side dish for cold winter days. There are 4 liberal portions in this recipe for only 35 calories each. It is also a good evening snack when the dieter looks as though he will never last until breakfast.

PICKLED MUSHROOMS

1 quart cider vinegar
1 lemon, sliced
1 teaspoon salt
¼ cup chili sauce
⅓ cup allspice
2 pounds button mush-
rooms

I suggest using button mushrooms because they look so nice and are the ideal size for pickling. You can use regular sized mushrooms, however, and simply slice them rather thin.

Combine all the ingredients, *except* the mushrooms, in a saucepan and bring to a boil. Then add the mushrooms and bring to a second boil. Remove from the heat. Pack into jars and refrigerate. The mushrooms can be kept up to 3 weeks (if they last that long).

The entire recipe is 185 calories. Happy nibbling!

MUSHROOMS STROGANOFF

1 tablespoon sour cream
½ cup buttermilk
1 tablespoon butter
¾ cup minced onion
1½ pounds mushrooms,
sliced
1¼ teaspoons salt
¼ teaspoon freshly
ground pepper
2 teaspoons paprika

Blend the sour cream and buttermilk and set aside.

Melt the butter in a preheated skillet and sauté the onions for about 5 minutes. Add the mushrooms, salt and pepper, and sauté until the mushrooms are browned. There should be no liquid in the pan at this time. Blend in the paprika and buttermilk mixture and heat thoroughly without boiling.

Serves 4 to 6 as a side dish. For 4, the calorie content per serving is 82.

MUSHROOMS AND GREEN PEPPERS

2 teaspoons olive oil
1 cup thinly sliced onions
2 green peppers, cut in rings
½ pound mushrooms, sliced
1¼ teaspoons salt
¼ teaspoon freshly ground pepper
⅛ teaspoon oregano

Preheat a pan and add the oil. Sauté onions covered for 2 minutes and uncovered for 3 minutes. Add the green pepper and sauté for 5 minutes, stirring frequently. Add the mushrooms, salt, pepper and oregano, and cook for about 6 minutes, until the mushrooms are tender.

This will serve 4, with a calorie count of about 45 per serving. It is particularly good with an omelette or fish.

EASY GOURMET MUSHROOMS

½ cup boiling water
1 tablespoon shallots or chives
½ teaspoon steak sauce
1 envelope beef bouillon
1 pound mushroom caps
1 tablespoon powdered flour
3 tablespoons skimmed evaporated milk (page 3)

Bring the water and shallots or chives rapidly to a boil. Then add the steak sauce and your favorite beef bouillon (not consommé—that has added calories and does little to enhance the flavor). When the bouillon has dissolved, add the mushroom caps and simmer for about 15 minutes. Then add the flour and stir until thickened (about another 5 minutes). Just before serving, add the milk and warm thoroughly.

This is a good side dish for 4 and a great luncheon for 2 on a bed of cooked rice (2 tablespoons of cooked rice each).

There are 36 calories per serving if you are serving 4.

MUSHROOM SOUFFLÉ

½ pound mushrooms
2 tablespoons butter or
margarine
¼ cup flour

½ teaspoon salt
few grains pepper
1 cup milk
3 egg yolks

3 egg whites

Clean the mushrooms and chop fine. Brown lightly in butter or margarine. Blend in flour, salt and pepper. Add milk gradually; cook, stirring constantly, until thick. Cool. Beat egg yolks well; add. Beat egg whites stiff, but not dry; fold in. Pour into greased baking dish; bake in moderate oven (325°) for 50 minutes. Serve immediately.

This dish is impressive and tastes wonderful. You can serve 3 for lunch at 224 calories each or use it as a side dish for 6.

BAKED STUFFED MUSHROOMS

24 large mushrooms
1 tablespoon vegetable oil
½ cup chopped onion
¼ cup chopped green
pepper
¾ teaspoon salt

¼ teaspoon freshly
ground black pepper
3 tablespoons grated
Parmesan cheese
1 tablespoon bread
crumbs

olive oil

Wash and dry the mushrooms. Remove the stems and chop fine. Heat vegetable oil in a skillet; sauté the onion and green pepper covered for 5 minutes. Add the chopped stems; sauté 5 minutes. Mix in the salt, pepper, cheese and bread crumbs; stuff the mushrooms with the mixture. Place in an oiled baking dish and sprinkle 1 drop of olive oil on each mushroom. Bake in a 375° oven for 15 minutes.

These mushrooms are quite versatile. They can be used as a side dish, for hors d'oeuvres, or as a main dish for lunch. In any case, each mushroom has 15 calories.

TOMATO-ONION SCALLOP

2 cups thinly sliced onions
2 teaspoons butter
2 slices toast, cubed
3 cups chopped peeled tomatoes
1 teaspoon salt
freshly ground pepper to taste
1 teaspoon sugar
2 tablespoons minced green pepper
2 tablespoons Parmesan cheese

Sauté the onions in the butter in a preheated pan until they are tender. You may have to cover the pan for a few minutes because you are using such a small amount of fat. When the onions are tender, place them in a baking dish. Toss the toast cubes in the tomatoes with the salt, pepper and sugar. Pour this mixture over the onions. Sprinkle with minced green pepper and Parmesan cheese, and bake in a 350° oven for about 35 minutes.

This will give 6 people a hearty side dish at 82 calories each and could make a very good luncheon dish, too.

TURNIPS ORIENTALE

8 medium turnips, peeled and grated
2 tablespoons oil
½ teaspoon salt
1 cup beef bouillon
½ cup sliced scallions
¼ teaspoon black pepper
1 tablespoon soy sauce

Sauté the turnips in the oil for 2 minutes covered and for 1 minute uncovered, stirring constantly. Add the salt and bouillon and bring to a boil. Bring the heat down to a simmer and cook, covered, for 5 minutes. Add the scallions and black pepper and soy sauce. Cook uncovered for 3 minutes.

This is an interesting change-of-pace side dish. You get 4 good portions for 70 calories each.

VEGETARIAN STUFFED CABBAGE

1 head of cabbage	½ teaspoon Worcester-
1 cup boiling water	shire sauce
1 tablespoon plus 1 tea-	8 tablespoons cooked rice
spoon oil	1½ teaspoons salt
½ cup chopped onions	¼ teaspoon fresh ground
½ pound mushrooms,	pepper
sliced	1 cup tomato sauce

Cover the cabbage with boiling water and let it stand for 10 minutes to soften the leaves. Remove 16 good leaves. Heat 1 teaspoon oil in a preheated saucepan and sauté the onions and mushrooms for 10 minutes. Mix in the Worcestershire sauce, rice, salt and pepper. Place 1 tablespoon of the mixture on each leaf, turn in the ends and roll up the leaf.

Shred half the remaining cabbage and spread it in a casserole. Put the cabbage rolls on the shredded cabbage and cover with 1 tablespoon of oil mixed with the tomato sauce. Bake covered in a 350° oven for 45 minutes; then uncover and bake 15 minutes longer.

Each of the rolls plus some of the sauce has 28 calories. (Of course, the dieter can go easy on the sauce because it contains oil, which accounts for a good number of the calories.)

You'll have some leftover shredded cabbage. Drain it well and toss some of it into your salads for the next few days.

VEGETABLE SOUFFLÉ

3 cups mashed vegetables	1 tablespoon powdered
3 eggs, separated	flour
salt and pepper to taste	

Do not include lima beans in the mashed vegetables, nor more than 1 medium potato, nor more than ½ cup of green peas. By all means, include celery (cooked), green pepper, at least 1 onion, carrots, asparagus and any other low-calorie vegetable you can think of or have around.

Mash the vegetables as thoroughly as possible by putting them through a ricer or food mill. Mix them with the egg yolks and flour and add salt and pepper. Beat the egg whites until stiff (you may add an extra egg if you wish) and fold them into the vegetable mixture. Pour into a greased casserole, soufflé dish or loaf pan. Preheat the oven to 375° and bake for 30 minutes. Serve immediately.

This serves 6 as a side dish at 75 calories per portion.

ZUCCHINI À NEIL

1 pound zucchini   salt and freshly ground
2 large onions, sliced   pepper to taste
1 tablespoon margarine

Soak, brush and clean the zucchini thoroughly because they may be sandy and nothing can spoil food as much as the gritty feel of sand when you chew!

Slice the zucchini in ¼-in round pieces. Slice the onions in very thin slices. Heat the skillet (use one that has a cover), put in the margarine and then the onions. Fry the onions slowly until they are golden. Place the zucchini on top of the onions and add salt and pepper. Cover the skillet and steam the zucchini until they are tender, turning them from time to time.

These are so good that we often consider them the main attraction of our meal. You can get 4 good portions, with each one only 50 calories.

Desserts

DESSERT TOPPING

There are a few commercial low-calorie toppings on the market. Because the toppings seem to vary in different areas, let me recommend the following recipe which I have used:

Almost freeze a suitable amount of skimmed evaporated milk (page 3), then whip it. Remember that you get a very large amount when it is whipped; since it cannot be stored successfully, make only enough for one serving. One quarter cup will do for 4 to 6 servings. Put the milk in the freezer in a bowl large enough to be used for beating. When the milk is almost frozen, remove it, whip it with a rotary beater, adding one or a combination of the following:

sugar substitute equal to 2 tablespoons sugar

¼ teaspoon almond or vanilla extract

1 tablespoon brandy or cognac

1 tablespoon chocolate syrup

I'm sure you'll be able to add to this list.

There are 50 calories in ¼ cup of skimmed

milk and 50 calories in the chocolate syrup. The calorie content of the other ingredients is negligible.

ORANGE BAVARIAN CREAM

½ cup skimmed evaporated milk (page 3)
1 tablespoon unflavored gelatin
¼ cup cold water
¾ cup orange juice
2 tablespoons lemon juice

½ teaspoon grated orange rind
sugar substitute equal to ⅓ cup sugar
¼ teaspoon salt
1 egg white
1 tablespoon sugar

Use a bowl large enough for whipping; place the milk in the freezer until it is almost frozen, then whip it. Sprinkle the gelatin in the cold water and let it soak a few minutes. Heat the fruit juices and the orange rind with the sugar substitute and dissolve the gelatin in the hot fruit juice. Chill until it is partially set. Salt the egg white and beat until stiff. Add the sugar and continue beating until it is glossy. Fold the egg white into the whipped milk and then combine both with the gelatin. Pour into individual dessert dishes and chill. This does not keep well, so it is best to make just what you will need for the day.

This is enough for 6 and each portion has 50 calories.

FRUIT WHIP

⅔ cup fruit pulp
1 tablespoon lemon juice
2 egg whites
¼ teaspoon salt

1 tablespoon sugar
sugar substitute equal to 3 tablespoons sugar

To make the fruit pulp, mash, sieve or grate your favorite fruit or berry, then add the lemon juice. Beat the egg whites with salt until they are stiff and then add the sugar and the sugar substitute slowly. Fold in the fruit pulp and pour into individual dessert cups. Chill. Use the same day.

This is a light dessert and each of 4 portions has only 44 calories.

SILVER DOLLARS

8 tablespoons skimmed milk cottage cheese (½ cup)

1 egg

sugar substitute equal to 1 tablespoon sugar

¼ teaspoon cinnamon

1 tablespoon powdered flour

1 pinch salt

¼ teaspoon vanilla

1 teaspoon butter

Sieve the cottage cheese or beat it with a rotary beater or put it in the blender so that you get a softer, creamy consistency. Beat the egg with all the remaining ingredients except the butter and mix them together until well blended.

Add ½ teaspoon of butter to a coated frying pan that has been preheated and drop in the batter with a tablespoon (the size will approximate that of a silver dollar). Fry at a moderate heat until golden and then turn.

This amount of batter will yield about 12 silver dollars at only 20 calories each. I serve this for dessert when I have a fish dinner. These silver dollars can be served *with* the fish by eliminating the cinnamon, sugar and vanilla, and substituting 1 small minced onion, white pepper and 2 pinches of salt. Sauté the onion in a little oil until golden brown and then add it to the creamed cottage cheese. This is a good dish for summer or winter menus.

BISQUIT TORTONI

1 cup water

1 cup nonfat dry milk

¼ cup lemon juice

1 tablespoon sugar

sugar substitute equal to ½ cup sugar

1 tablespoon sherry

½ tablespoon almond extract

½ teaspoon vanilla extract

2 tablespoons ground almonds

Beat the water and the milk until the mixture begins to thicken. Add the lemon juice and beat until this mixture is thick. Next add the sugar and sugar substitute and continue beating until the mixture is as thick as cream. Fold in the sherry and the extracts and spoon into paper cups (4-ounce size). Sprinkle the almonds on top and freeze. Delicious!

This makes about 8 portions and you might get 10. If we count on 10 portions each one will have 86 calories and you can hardly tell it's a fake!

CRUST FOR CHEESECAKES

There are two methods you can use in making this low-calorie crust. Both involve the use of vanilla wafers of which you need about 10.

In the first method you must grease the pan lightly with butter and then put the wafers in a food mill. Hold the mill over the pan and as you work it the crumbs will fall into the pan. From time to time you can move the pan around so that it gets evenly coated. The crumbs will only stick on the buttered surface so you can pour off any excess. With this method you will be using the least amount of crackers, thereby getting the least amount of calories. You will even have some left over to sprinkle on top of your cake.

With the second method you have to put the wafers through the food mill also, but you then mix them with 2 tablespoons of nonfat dry milk and cut in 1 tablespoon of butter. This is all mashed together and then flattened against the sides and bottom of the pan. The shell has to be frozen and is good to use with a refrigerator cake. When you pour the filling into this shell, the shell will adhere to it and give a good crust (almost like the high-calorie variety!).

Ten cookies will cover about a 10-inch pan and the entire crust will have 150 calories.

FRUIT CHEESECAKE

½ cup skimmed evapo-
  rated milk (page 3)
4 tablespoons lemon juice
6 tablespoons water
sugar substitute equal to
  ½ cup sugar

1 envelope unflavored
  gelatin
1 cup cottage cheese
½ teaspoon vanilla
1 cup well-drained dietetic
  fruit cocktail

Place the skimmed evaporated milk in the
freezer before you do anything else. The milk has
to be almost frozen to be used in this recipe. Mix
the lemon juice with the water, sugar substitute
and gelatin. Cook and stir until the gelatin dissolves, then cool. Put the cheese through a sieve
or the blender and beat until smooth. Stir in the
gelatin mixture and the vanilla, blending well.
Chill until partially set.

When the cheese sets, whip the frozen milk
until it peaks. Fold the fruit into the partially set
cheese, then fold in the whipped milk. Spoon into
a spring pan or a square cake pan and refrigerate
overnight.

If you like, you can grease the pan very lightly
and sprinkle it with vanilla wafer crumbs. I make
mine by putting the wafers through a food mill.
If you use 10 wafers, you'll have enough crumbs
for the sides, bottom and even some to sprinkle
on top.

This cheesecake will serve 6 at 55 calories per
serving without the crumbs. With the crumbs, add
another 25 calories per serving.

STRAWBERRY CHEESECAKE

1½ cups cottage cheese
3 eggs
¼ teaspoon salt
½ teaspoon almond
  extract

1 tablespoon sugar
sugar substitute equal to 3
  tablespoons sugar
strawberries

Cream the cottage cheese by putting it through a sieve and then beating it with a rotary beater. Or you can whip it through your blender. Beat in the eggs, salt, almond extract and sugars. Pour this mixture into a buttered (just lightly, now) 9-inch pan and bake in a preheated oven at 350°. Cool and then garnish with fresh strawberries that have been covered with sugar substitute.

Don't be disappointed when the cake comes out of the oven rather flat. It will taste good anyway and the 6 ample portions have 92 calories each.

COTTAGE CHEESE MOUSSE

½ pound cottage cheese
4 egg yolks
2 teaspoons confectioners sugar

sugar substitute equal to ½ cup sugar
1 teaspoon Grand Marnier

Be sure to separate the egg whites and yolks very carefully; if the white gets into the yolk, the consistency of the mousse will be too loose. Pass the cheese through a sieve and cream it. Beat the egg yolks with the sugar, sugar substitute and liqueur until the consistency is thick and creamy. Whip the egg yolks and the cheese together. Spoon into dessert cups or a small mold. Chill until thoroughly firm. Unmold and either dribble grenadine over it or serve with fresh berries.

This refreshing, delectable dessert will serve 6, and each serving contains 80 calories.

STRAWBERRY BAVARIAN CREAM

½ cup skimmed evaporated milk (page 3)
2 cups crushed strawberries
1 tablespoon confectioners sugar
1 envelope unflavored gelatin

2 tablespoons water
1 cup strawberry juice or water
1 pinch salt
sugar substitute equal to ½ cup sugar
1 tablespoon lemon juice

Place the skimmed milk in the freezer in a bowl large enough for whipping. Crush the strawberries and sprinkle with confectioners sugar. Let this stand while you soak the gelatin in 2 tablespoons of water for 5 minutes. Place over boiling water and stir steadily until the gelatin dissolves. Combine the gelatin with the berries, juice (or water), salt, sugar substitute and lemon juice. Blend all these ingredients well and chill until partially set.

When the milk in the freezer is almost frozen solid, remove and whip. Fold the whipped milk into the berry mixture and divide into 8 to 10 individual serving dishes or into a large mold. Chill well and garnish with fresh berries.

If you serve this to 8, each portion will have 41 calories.

SHERBET??

6 tablespoons cottage cheese	1 envelope unflavored gelatin
1 cup buttermilk	¼ cup cold water
1 teaspoon almond flavoring	¾ cup hot water

Put the cheese through a sieve or blender so that it is creamed. Blend it with the buttermilk and almond flavoring. Soften the gelatin in cold water for 5 minutes and then add the hot water and stir until the gelatin is dissolved. Place this in a pan of ice cubes and stir steadily until the water begins to thicken. Combine the gelatin and the cheese mixture and chill in individual dessert cups. Garnish with a little fresh fruit, or dribble some noncaloric fruit-flavored soda on it.

This "sherbet" is in no way related to the common variety found in the frozen food bins. However, it is also unrelated calorically: 20 calories per portion for 6!

CHESTNUT HONEY TREATS

1 pound chestnuts (about 50)
4 tablespoons honey
½ teaspoon powdered ginger (optional)
1 teaspoon cinnamon
2 tablespoons powdered sugar or 2 tablespoons chopped almonds

Cut a cross on the top of each chestnut. Boil for 30 minutes, then peel and grind the nuts. Cut in the honey and add the other ingredients, *except* the sugar and almonds. Form into small balls and sprinkle with the powdered sugar or chopped almonds. You'll get about 25 balls and each one has about 22 calories.

They are very sweet and satisfying so you can't eat too many. (I can hear you saying, "Who can't?")

LEMON CHIFFON MOLD

2 envelopes unflavored gelatin
1½ cups water
⅛ teaspoon salt
sugar substitute equal to ½ cup sugar
6 ounces low-calorie lemon or lime concentrate, frozen *
1 teaspoon almond extract
½ cup skimmed evaporated milk (page 3)

Sprinkle gelatin on 1 cup of water in a 2½-quart saucepan. Stir and cook until dissolved (this takes about 3 minutes). Remove saucepan from heat, stir in salt and sugar substitute and add frozen concentrate, ½ cup of water and the almond extract. Place the skimmed evaporated milk in a bowl large enough for whipping and place in the freezer for about 20 minutes (until almost frozen). Whip until it peaks. Mix gelatin and defrosted concentrate well. Fold in the whipped milk and turn into a 6-cup mold. Chill until firm.

_____

* Six tablespoons reconstituted lemon or lime juice plus enough water to make ¾ cup of liquid. To this add a sugar substitute equal to ½ cup sugar.

This will serve 6 at only 30 calories, so you can encourage your companion to have a second helping.

PARISIENNE FRUITS

¼ cup skimmed evapo-
rated milk (page 3)
3 beaten egg whites

½ teaspoon vanilla
sugar substitute equal to
¼ cup sugar

3 cups berries, washed, drained and sprinkled
with an artificial sweetner

Place the milk into a container that can be used for whipping and put it into the freezer; it has to remain there until it is almost frozen. Beat the egg whites until they are stiff and whip the frozen milk until it has the consistency of whipped cream. While you are whipping the milk, add the vanilla and sugar substitute. Fold the milk into the beaten egg whites. The next step is to fold in the berries. If they are small or soft, you may leave them whole; if not, you can crush or slice them. The fruit is to be folded in last. Spoon into individual serving dishes and serve immediately. Top with a whole berry.

These 8 portions have 40 calories each.

CHOCOLATE PUDDING

1 cup skimmed evaporated
milk (page 3)
1 envelope unflavored
gelatin
sugar substitute equal to 1
cup sugar

⅛ teaspoon salt
1 egg yolk
¾ cup skimmed milk
2 ounces liquid baking
chocolate
1 teaspoon vanilla

The evaporated milk will have to be whipped when it is almost frozen, so put it in a bowl large enough for beating and place it in the freezer. Do this first. Mix the gelatin, sugar substitute and salt thoroughly. Beat the egg yolk and the skimmed milk and add to the gelatin mixture. Put in the chocolate and cook over medium heat, stirring continuously until all ingredients are blended. Be careful not to boil. Beat smooth with a rotary beater. Chill in the refrigerator, stirring occasionally, until the mixture becomes very thick but not hardened. Whip the evaporated milk with the vanilla and fold it into the pudding mixture. Pour into individual dessert cups and chill.

Serves 8 for 55 calories each. This resembles a mousse somewhat and is a welcome change for the dieter if you can't get a commercial low-calorie pudding in your community.

PUDDIN' PIE

½ pound cottage cheese
4 eggs, separated
sugar substitute equal to ½ cup sugar
1 tablespoon flour
¼ teaspoon lemon flavoring
¼ teaspoon vanilla
salt

Let the cheese stand at room temperature for about an hour in the winter and less in the summer. Then sieve it or put it through a blender. Cream the cheese and the egg yolks together. Blend them thoroughly, adding the sugar substitute, flour and flavorings. Beat the egg whites until stiff and fold into the cheese. Pour this into a 10-inch pie shell and bake at 400° for 25 to 30 minutes.

This will serve 6 at 85 calories per serving.

RICE PUDDING

1 cup cooked rice
cinnamon to taste
1 tablespoon butter
3 cups skimmed milk
nutmeg to taste

Mix all the ingredients and pour into a greased casserole (use some of the butter to grease the casserole). Bake at 325° for 1 hour. This is rich, creamy and very satisfying. Each of 6 servings contains 92 calories.

I use regular rice for this recipe, but there is an imported rice that is lower in calories.

MINNA'S NOODLE PUDDING

4 ounces cottage cheese
1 cup buttermilk
¼ teaspoon salt
sugar substitute equal to 6
   tablespoons sugar

¼ teaspoon cinnamon
1 egg, separated (use an
   extra white if you have
   it)
1 tablespoon butter

1 cup cooked broad egg noodles

Put the cheese through a sieve or blender and then whip it with the buttermilk. Add the salt, sugar substitute, cinnamon and egg yolk and beat until the mixture is creamy. Beat the egg white or whites until stiff. Melt the butter in the casserole to grease it and pour the remainder onto the noodles. Combine the noodles and the cheese, blending well; fold in the egg whites and pour into the casserole. Bake, uncovered, for 1 hour at 325° and then keep in the oven for another ½ hour. Serve warm or cold. Each of 6 portions is 76 calories.

APPLE PUDDING

2 cups Puffed Rice
sugar substitute equal to 4
   tablespoons sugar
1 tablespoon melted
   butter
¼ teaspoon cinnamon

1 large apple, sliced thin
2 teaspoons brown sugar
½ teaspoon vanilla
½ cup skimmed milk
nutmeg

Crush the Puffed Rice with a rolling pin or in a blender. Mix it with the low-calorie sweetener, butter and cinnamon. Place ⅓ of the Puffed Rice in a small casserole, cover with ⅓ of the sliced apples and sprinkle with some of the brown sugar. Repeat this until everything is used up. Gently pour the vanilla and milk over all. Sprinkle with nutmeg and bake uncovered at 350° for 1 hour. Serve warm.

This is a filling dessert for 4 at 85 calories each.

CHEESE N' CHIVE PUDDING

butter   4 tablespoons chives
6 ounces cottage cheese   pepper to taste
2 eggs   ¼ teaspoon salt
                  1 tablespoon flour

Use just enough butter to grease a 1½-quart casserole. Start warming the oven at 300°. Cream the cottage cheese by any of these three methods: Put it through a sieve or a blender or beat it with a rotary beater. Separate the eggs, reserving the whites. Blend the yolks, cheese and all other ingredients until the mixture is a creamy paste. Beat whites until stiff but still moist, and then fold them into the cheese mixture. Bake for 1 hour and serve immediately. As a side dish, this will yield 4 ample portions at 80 calories each.

More Food Suggestions

There are a few treats that you can allow your dieter. You must, however, be very careful about the quantities; they *must* be limited.

Cocoa:
You can serve 1 tablespoon of cocoa with 1 cup of skimmed milk and a sugar substitute to taste for a grand total of 105 calories. This is particularly good for the child dieter.

Cheese Tidbits:
These can be offered with a glass of dry white wine before dinner; 3 ounces of wine and 10 tidbits total 85 calories.

Marshmallows:
You can offer 3. They are 30 calories each.

Popcorn:
Be magnanimous—give him a cup. Use no butter, just the specified amount of oil for popping and season with salt and pepper or with seasoned salt, garlic salt (this is good for parties) or onion salt. One cup popped has 50 calories.

Apple Butter:
Each tablespoon contains 35 calories. If your dieter has a sweet tooth, you can serve 1 tablespoon

of apple butter over 2 tablespoons of cottage cheese. It makes a good dessert—65 calories for both.

Chestnuts:

There are 50 calories in 10 chestnuts. These are particularly good to offer because peeling them takes time; they are hot, filling and oh so good on a cold winter's night.

Candies:

1 sourball is 30 calories.
1 small piece of peanut brittle is 50 calories.
1 caramel is 50 calories.
1 Mallomar is 61 calories, if it's the last one in the box.

On Being a Good Companion

Don't advertise (to friends) that the dieter is at it again: dieting.

Don't nag him about what he should and should not eat, especially when you are in company. Allow him the privilege of being responsible for his own food choices. As a companion you are in charge of the meals *you* serve.

Have only low-calorie foods on hand, BUT have plenty!

Expect displays of extreme vanity, such as prolonged looks in the mirror from all angles. Run into the kitchen and laugh there; don't embarrass the dieter.

Be profuse in your praise of his willpower, judgment—anything.

After one week of dieting, be sure to find one spot where he appears thinner and mention it, almost casually.

Don't act like a martyr because you have to learn a whole new way of cooking and living. You'll get no sympathy from the dieter. After all, he is making the supreme sacrifice: he feels he is losing a part of his physical self and who can argue with that!

Be encouraging at all times, even when he is in the midst of a binge.

This is important! Remember: have one food per meal that the dieter can eat in unlimited quantity.

And by all means, when times get a little rough, run to your favorite hiding place and munch through a box of chocolate Mallomars.

Ammunition Foods

Keep plenty of these foods handy. They are satisfying and contain very few calories—you can eat all you want!

beets (and greens)	lettuce
broccoli	mushrooms
brussels sprouts	onions
cabbage	parsley
cauliflower	pickles
celery	radishes
chard	raw peppers
clams	sauerkraut
cucumbers	spinach
dandelion greens	string beans
gelatin (unsweetened)	tomato juice
leeks	watercress

Comforting Foods

These foods are of relatively low caloric content and are more "filling" than Ammunition Foods. You can't eat *all* you want—but these are great for fighting off that urge . . .

apples	lobster
apricots	mussels
artichokes	pears
asparagus	pot cheese
cantaloupe	scallops
carrots	shrimp
chestnuts	strawberries
chicken	tangerines
cottage cheese	tomatoes
egg plant	tongue
grapefruit	veal
lean beefburgers	

. . . and for Special Comfort, drink

bouillon   coffee   tea

"Poison" Foods

These foods are tagged with this warning label to remind you to keep away from them; they are high in calories and are destructively dangerous to you!

ale
avocado
baked apple (sugared)
baked beans
beer
bread—in excess
butter—in excess
cake
candies
chocolate
cookies
cream
cream cheese
creamed soups
dates
doughnuts
dressings
dried fruits
duck
fat meats
goose
gravies
griddle cakes
ice cream
jams
jellies
macaroni
malted milk
nuts
peanut butter
pie
pizza
spaghetti
sugar—in excess

Index